ALL-IN-ONE **SPANISH** LEARNING GUIDE

A complete step-by-step method to practice your listening and pronunciation

Also available:

Spanish Grammar for Beginners (https://geni.us/spanishgrambeg)

Spanish Short Stories for Beginners (https://geni.us/spanishbookbeginner)

Spanish Phrase Book (https://geni.us/spanishphrase)

TABLE OF CONTENTS

INTRODUCTION

So, you've decided to teach yourself Spanish. *¡Qué bien!* I'm sure you've thought long and hard before taking the plunge, given that everyone seems to think that learning Spanish on your own is impossible. Truth is, it's not! It is actually a very attainable goal. All you need is the right amount of motivation, a healthy learning habit, and the right tools and resources to make your Spanish-speaking dreams come true.

And, lucky you, you've come to the right place. We're here to provide you with all the language-learning resources you'll need. The motivation part is up to you, though. But, seeing as our goal at My Daily Spanish is to make learning Spanish fun and enjoyable so as to help bolster your motivation, we've created this book specifically with you in mind.

In this book, you will find a complete step-by-step learning method to get you speaking Spanish in no time!

How does this book work?

In this book, you will find twenty lessons. Each lesson is designed to be tackled in a day. Five days a week, for four weeks, and you're done! Doesn't sound bad at all, does it?

Each lesson will contain:

- One to three grammar topics
- Sample dialogue to illustrate grammar points
- Audio recorded by native Spanish speakers for you to listen to, follow along, and guides you to help you learn the pronunciations
  Important note: The link to download the audio files is available at the end of this book. (Page 236)
- Exercises and practice activities
  Important note: The answer key for each exercise is provided at the end of the lesson.
- Vocabulary lists
- And more!

Each lesson will be short enough to hold your interest but still challenging enough to give your brain a good workout.

What makes this book different?

There are so many books out there promising to teach you Spanish. So, how do you know you've chosen the right one?

The answer is simple: **the method.**

This book was written just for you: the independent learner. You will be provided with everything you need to begin a successful journey toward speaking Spanish.

A strong focus on listening

Each grammar point you learn will be illustrated through a conversation, spoken by native Spanish speakers. You will hear the language being used in a natural, authentic way. This will help the grammar and vocabulary become more solidified in your mind, as well as train your ear and improve your pronunciation.

Build a learning habit

If you have visited our website www.mydailyspanish.com, you know that we believe in building a Spanish habit.

Learning a language is something that takes time and dedication. This book hopes to give you both the motivation and the resources you need in order to be successful in not only learning Spanish, but in making it a part of your everyday life.

The lessons will last 20–30 minutes, and at the end of each, you will walk away with a better understanding of the language. Allocating time each day to learn a language is crucial. And, through this book, as well as other materials we have available online, you will be able to incorporate Spanish into your life in an easy and enjoyable way that isn't too overwhelming, no matter how much time you choose to spend on it.

Is this book for you?

If you are a beginner (i.e. no previous knowledge of Spanish at all) then yes, this book is most definitely for you! It will even serve those who have studied Spanish in the past, but want to get back to basics and refresh their memories before diving even deeper into the language.

More specifically, this book was written with you, the student, in mind. The grammar explanations have been written out carefully, so that anyone can understand them (even if you don't have a Spanish teacher on hand to ask for help). The goal of this book is to help learners who are embarking on this journey on their own. If this is you, don't worry! You are not as alone as you may think. We are all in this together at Mydailyspanish.com!

What can you expect out of this book?

After a month of learning Spanish with this book, you will:

- Have a working understanding of the language (noun genders, adjectives, verb conjugations, etc.)
- Be able to talk about yourself, your family, and your friends (descriptions – both physical and in terms of personality)
- Be able to discuss your day-to-day life
- Know how to have basic conversations in Spanish
- Learn a ton of new, useful vocabulary you can use daily
- Have the confidence to get out there and start putting your language abilities to the test!

So, what are we waiting for? *¡Vamos a aprender español!* (Let's learn Spanish!)

Thank you,

My Daily Spanish Team

PLEASE READ!

The link to download the audio files is available at the end of this book. (Page 236)

The answer key for each exercise is provided at the end of the lesson.

Week 1, Day 1: Basic Greetings

What's in store for you today: Basic Greetings

Vocabulary: Basic Greetings

Listen to Track 1.1.1

Woman: *Hola. ¿Cómo estás?* (Hello, how are you?)

Girl: *Buenos días. Estoy bien. ¿Y usted?* (Good day. I'm fine, and you?)

Woman: *Estoy bien, gracias.* (I'm fine, thank you.)

Girl: *¿Cómo se llama?* (What is your name?)

Woman: *Me llamo Señora González. ¿Y tú? ¿Cómo te llamas?* (My name is Señora González. And you? What is your name?)

Girl: *Me llamo Lucía.* (My name is Lucía.)

Woman: *Hasta luego, Lucía.* (See you later, Lucía.)

Girl: *Adiós, Señora González.* (Goodbye, Señora González.)

Let's start by looking at some basic greetings.

Standard/Formal Greetings

Listen to Track 1.1.2

As you probably already know, "***hola***" is a very common greeting in Spanish. It means "**hello**" and can be used any time you would use this everyday salutation. If you want to be more specific, though, and say something like "**good day**" or "**good afternoon**," you have some options for that. And here they are:

- When you see someone earlier in the day, you'll say, "***buenos días,***" which is like saying "**good day.**"
- When you see someone in the afternoon or evening, you'll say, "***buenas tardes,***" which is like saying "**good afternoon/good evening.**"

Listen to Track 1.1.3

When you want to say "goodbye," you can, of course, use the traditional *"adiós"* that everyone knows so well. But if you want to switch it up a little, here are some options you can choose from.

- *Hasta Luego*: This means, "**until later**" and is a very common farewell in Spain.
- *Hasta La Próxima*: This is like saying **"until next time."**
- *Chao* (pronounced like the Italian *"ciao"*) is another common way of saying **"goodbye"** in Spain.
- *Hasta mañana*: "**Until tomorrow.**"
- *Hasta pronto*: "**Until soon.**" You would use this if you know you'll see the person again within a short span of time.
- *Nos vemos*: This is similar to saying "**see ya.**"

Something a little more informal

As you will soon learn, there is often a formal and an informal way of saying things in Spanish. Sometimes the difference is grammatical, while other times, it's simply in your choice of words. The phrase *"buenas,"* for example, is one of those "choice of words" moments.

"Buenas" is a quick, easy, informal way of saying "**hello.**" You can use it at any time of day, and it's pretty easy to remember, too!

Listening and Practice

Listen to each of the following greetings being said, in order, by a native Spanish speaker. Really pay attention to how the words sound. Take note of any sounds that surprise you, or sound different than you had imagined the words being said.

It's time to start training your ear!

Listen to Track 1.1.4

- *Hola* – Hello
- *Buenos días* – Good morning
- *Buenas tardes* – Good afternoon
- *Buenas noches* – Good night

- ***Adiós*** – Goodbye
- ***Hasta mañana*** – See you tomorrow
- ***Hasta luego*** – See you later
- ***Hasta pronto*** – See you soon
- ***Hasta la próxima*** – Until next time
- ***Nos vemos*** - See ya

Of course, after you say "**hello**" to someone, you're probably going to want to continue the conversation. Why not ask them their name? Below, you'll see how to do that in both the formal and informal contexts.

> **Note:** Before we get too far along with all this "**formal/informal**" stuff, let's discuss what we mean when we make this distinction. A good rule of thumb is this: if you're around someone you don't know, or someone you would address with a title (**Mr., Mrs., Dr., etc.**), you'll probably use the formal option. Informal is usually reserved for friends and family.

Listen to Track 1.1.5

In a formal situation, you'll ask:

- *¿Cómo se llama?* (What is your name?)
- Or *¿Cuál es su nombre?* (What is your name?)

In an informal situation, you'll ask:

- *¿Cómo te llamas?* (What is your name?)
- *¿Cuál es tu nombre?* (What is your name?)

And the answer will be either:

- *Me llamo...* (My name is...)
- *Mi nombre es...* (My name is...)

Listen to Track 1.1.6

And, just because we're being nice here, let's talk about ways to say "**it's nice to meet you.**" You have a few options here, so take your pick!

- *Es un placer conocerle* (It's a pleasure to meet you – formal.)
- *Es un placer conocerte* (It's a pleasure to meet you – informal.)
- *Encantada* (Pleased to meet you. - feminine)
- *Encantado* (Pleased to meet you. - masculine)
- *Mucho gusto* (Nice to meet you).

Listen to Track 1.1.7

In this little section, let's focus on asking how someone is doing. Again, here you have options for whether you want to be formal or informal in your question-asking.

In a formal situation:

- **You'll ask:** *¿Cómo está usted?*
- **A possible answer would be:** *Estoy bien, gracias.* (I'm fine, thank you.)

In an informal situation:

- **You'll ask:** *¿Cómo estás tú?*
- **A possible answer to your question would be:** *Así-así.* (So-so.)

Pronunciation and Vocabulary Practice

Let's take some time to practice your pronunciation and review the important vocabulary we've looked at so far.

For the following activities, listen to the tracks once. Then listen to them again, repeating what you hear. Focus not only on trying to mimic the pronunciation you hear in the recording but also on continuing to familiarize your ear with how Spanish sounds when spoken by a native speaker.

Listen to Track 1.1.8

Greetings and Farewells

Buenos días – Good morning / Good day

Buenas tardes – Good afternoon / Good evening

Adiós – Goodbye

Hasta luego – Until later

Listen to Track 1.1.9

In a Formal Situation

Buenos días. ¿Cómo está usted? – Good day. How are you?

Estoy bien, gracias. ¿Y usted? – I'm fine, thank you. And you?

Estoy muy bien. – I'm very well.

Adiós. – Goodbye.

Hasta luego. – Until later.

Listen to Track 1.1.10

In an Informal Situation

Hola, Sara. ¿Cómo estás? – Hello, Sara. How are you?

Bien. ¿Y tú? – Well, and you?

Estoy bien. – I'm fine.

Nos vemos. – See ya.

Hasta la próxima. – Until next time.

One last question:

- *¿Cómo se llama?* (**Formal**)
- *¿Cómo te llamas?* (**Informal**)

Practice Corner

Let's do some fill-in-the-blank activities to really solidify what you've just learned.

Exercise 1.1.1

Below you will see part of a conversation taking place between <u>strangers</u>. Fill in the missing words.

- **Sara**: _____________ *días, señor.* (_____________ morning , sir.)
- **Miguel**: *Hola, señora.* (Hello, ma'am.)
- **Sara**: *¿*_____________ *se llama?* (_____________ is your name?)
- **Miguel**: *Me llamo Miguel. ¿Y* _____________*?* (My name is Miguel and _____________?)
- **Sara**: *Me* _____________ *Sara.* (My _____________ is Sara.)
- **Miguel**: *Es un* _____________ *conocerle.* (It is a _____________ to know you.)
- **Sara**: *Encantada* (Nice to meet you)

Exercise 1.1.2

Now, let's try a conversation taking place between <u>friends</u>.

- **Ana**: *Hola, Juan. ¿Cómo* _____________*?* (Hello Juan. How are _____________?)
- **Juan**: *Hola, Ana. Estoy* _____________*, ¿y* _____*?* (Hello Ana. I am _____________, and _____?)
- **Ana**: *Muy* _____________*.* (Very _____________.)
- **Juan**: *Nos* _____________*.* (See _____________.)
- **Ana**: _____________ *mañana.* (_____________ tomorrow.)

Exercise 1.1.3

Now, let's try to make sure you know what means what. Translate the following expressions from English into Spanish:

Translation: Formal situation

- Hello, sir! _____________
- Hello, Julia. How are you today? _____________
- I'm fine. And you? _____________
- I'm fine, thank you. _____________

Translation: Informal situation

- Hello, Juan. _______________
- Hello, Lucía. _______________
- How are you? _______________
- Fine, and you? _______________
- So-so. _______________

Exercise 1.1.4

Write two sentences about yourself following the example:

Yo me llamo Ana. Yo soy de los Estados Unidos.

Additional Vocabulary:

Sometimes, you'll find an "**Additional Vocabulary**" section at the end of a lesson. This vocabulary is *optional*. It's good to know, but not part of our daily goals. So feel free to either study and learn these words, or simply skim through them.

Here are a few more useful greetings you might want to make a note of:

Listen to Track 1.1.11

Some casual greetings (to be used with friends):

- *¿Qué hay?* – What's up?
- *¿Qué pasa?* – What's happening?/What's up?
- *¿Qué tal?* – How's it going?
- *¡Hace mucho que no te veo!* – It's been a long time since I've seen you!
- *¿Cómo te va?* – How's it going?
- *¿Qué haces?* – What are you doing?

Some more answers to the question "¿Cómo estás?" (How are you?)

- *Un poco cansado* – A little tired (for men).
- *Un poco cansada* – A little tired (for women).
- *Estoy enfermo* – I'm sick (for men).

- ***Estoy enferma*** – I'm sick (for women).
- ***Más o menos*** – More or less.

Random things that are good to know:

- ***Nada*** – Nothing
- ***Lo siento*** – Sorry
- ***Chao*** – Goodbye
- ***Por favor*** – Please
- ***Gracias*** – Thank you
- ***Muchas gracias*** – Thank you very much
- ***De nada*** – You're welcome
- ***Yo no sé*** – I don't know
- ***Bienvenidos*** – Welcome

A Quick Recap of this Lesson

- We learned how to ask someone's name. (*¿Cómo te llamas? ¿Cómo se llama?*)
- We looked at how to ask someone how they're doing. (*¿Cómo estás? ¿Cómo está?*)
- And we learned how to answer these questions.
- We also had a little introduction to formal vs. informal speech in Spanish.

ANSWERS:

Exercise 1.1.1

- Sara: : ____Buenos_____ días, señor.
- Miguel: Hola, señora.
- Sara: ¿__Cómo__ se llama?
- Miguel: Me llamo Miguel. ¿Y __usted____?

- Sara: Me __llamo__ Sara.
- Miguel: Es un __placer__ conocerle.
- Sara: Encantada

Exercise 1.1.2

- Ana: Hola, Juan. ¿Cómo ____ estás__?
- Juan: Hola, Ana. Estoy ____ bien____, ¿y _tú_?

- Ana: Muy __bien__.
- Juan: Nos ____vemos____.
- Ana: ____Hasta__ mañana.

Exercise 1.1.3

Translation: Formal

- Hello, sir! – ¡Hola, señor!
- Hello, Julia. How are you? – Hola, Julia. ¿Cómo está usted?

- I'm fine. And you? – Estoy bien. ¿Y usted?
- I'm fine, thank you. – Estoy bien, gracias.

Translation: Informal

- Hello, Juan. – Hola, Juan.
- Hello, Lucía. – Hola, Lucía.
- How are you? – ¿Cómo estás?

- Fine, and you? – Bien, ¿y tú?
- So-so. – Así-así.

Week 1, Day 2: Spanish Alphabet

Listen to Track 1.2.1

Hombre: *Hola, me llamo Miguel Fernández. M-I-G-U-E-L F-E-R-N-A-N-D-E-Z*

(Hello, my name is Miguel Fernández.)

Mujer: *Hola, me llamo Verónica González. V-E-R-O-N-I-C-A G-O-N-Z-A-L-E-Z*

(Hello, my name is Verónica González.)

Pronunciation and Spelling – They go hand in hand

One thing about Spanish that a lot of students like is the fact that it's a "phonetic language." This means that when you see a word written down, you're going to pronounce it just as it's written. No "silent '*e*'s" like we have in English, or random letters in the middle of words that don't actually do anything (like the "*s*" in "island," for example).

So, if we're going to learn how to correctly pronounce things in Spanish, we should start by learning the letters. Today we're going to learn the Spanish alphabet!

The Alphabet

Listen to Track 1.2.2

Listen as a native speaker reads through the alphabet. Below, you will find the letters written out, but as their names and as they are pronounced.

Letter	Letter Name	Letter Pronunciation
A	a	ah
B	be	beh
C	ce	seh*
D	de	deh
E	e	eh
F	efe	eh-feh
G	ge	heh
H	hache	ah-cheh
I	i	ee
J	jota	hota
K	ka	ka
L	ele	el-lay
LL	elle	ey-yay
M	eme	eh-mey
N	ene	eh-nay
Ñ	eñe	eh-yay
O	o	o
P	pe	pay
Q	cu	koo
R	ere	er-ray
RR	erre	er-ray
S	ese	eh-say
T	te	tay
U	u	ooh

V	uve	oo-bay
W**	uve-doble	oo-bay-do-ble
X	equis	eh-kees
Y	i griega	e-gree-eh-ga
Z	zeta	seh-ta*

***Note:** In Spain, the way these letters are pronounced will be slightly different. "**C**", instead of being pronounced "**say**", will be pronounced "**thay**"; "**Z**" will be "**the-ta**."

****Note:** There are a few ways to say "**W**" in Spanish. Others include "**ve-doble**," "**doble-u**," and "**doble-ve**."

Exercise 1.2.1

Out of all the letters in the Spanish alphabet, the ones that tend to give students (especially English-speaking students) the most trouble are the vowels. Let's take some time to practice those right now, shall we?

Listen to Track 1.2.3

1. Listen as the speaker reads out the five vowels in a random order. Write them down as you listen and then check your answers:

_______ _______ _______ _______ _______

Listen to Track 1.2.4

2. Let's do the vowels one more time! Same activity, different order. We really want to make sure we get this down.

_______ _______ _______ _______ _______

Listen to Track 1.2.5

3. Listen as the speaker spells out three different words. Write down the letters you hear. When you finish, you'll have three useful new vocabulary words!

_______________ _______________ _______________

¿De dónde eres? - Where are you from?

Listen to Track 1.2.6

María: *Buenos días. Yo soy María.* (Good day. I am María.)

Jorge: *Hola, María. Yo me llamo Jorge.* (Hello, María. My name is Jorge.)

María: *¿De dónde eres, Jorge?* (Where are you from, Jorge?)

Jorge: *Soy de Madrid. ¿De dónde eres?* (I am from Madrid. Where are you from?)

María: *Yo soy de Barcelona.* (I am from Barcelona.)

Listen to Track 1.2.7

As with asking someone's name (**¿Cómo te llamas? ¿Cómo se llama**?) and how someone is doing (**¿Cómo estás? ¿Cómo está**?), there are two ways you can ask where someone is from. There are two ways you can ask where someone is from:

- Informal: *¿De dónde eres?* (Where are you from?)
- Formal: *¿De dónde es?* (Where are you from?)

To answer this question, you will say:

- *(Yo*) soy de...* (I am from...)

* The "yo" is optional.

Below, let's look at a list of 25 different countries in Spanish so you know how to answer the question when someone asks you! (Note: It's not necessary that you memorize all of these right now. But you may want to add them to your vocabulary list to study later.)

Listen to Track 1.2.8

- *Alemania* – Germany
- *Australia* – Australia
- *Bélgica* – Belgium
- *Brasil* – Brazil
- *Canadá* – Canada
- *China* – China
- *Colombia* – Colombia
- *Egipto* – Egypt
- *Inglaterra* – England
- *Francia* – France
- *Gales* – Wales
- *Grecia* – Greece

- ***Irlanda*** – (Republic of) Ireland
- ***Italia*** – Italy
- ***Japón*** – Japan
- ***Los Países Bajos*** – The Netherlands
- ***México*** – Mexico
- ***Polonia*** – Poland
- ***Portugal*** – Portugal
- ***Rusia*** – Russia
- ***Escocia*** – Scotland
- ***Sudáfrica*** – South Africa
- ***Corea del Sur*** – South Korea
- ***España*** – Spain
- ***El Reino Unido**** – The United Kingdom
- ***Los Estados Unidos*** – The United States

*When talking about this country, you're going to need to use a contraction. There are only two in Spanish, and we'll discuss them in more detail in the future. For now, just remember this:

- ***Yo soy del Reino Unido.*** (I am from the United Kingdom.)

Note:	Don't see your country? Check the additional vocabulary at the end of today's lesson. If it's still not there, get in touch with us, and we will resolve that!

Exercise 1.2.2

Write down the names of the countries as the speaker spells them.

Listen to Track 1.2.9

1. _______________________________
2. _______________________________
3. _______________________________
4. _______________________________
5. _______________________________

Practice Corner

Exercise 1.2.3

Listening:

Answer the following questions

Listen to Track 1.2.10

1. *¿Cómo se llama el hombre?* (What is the man's name?)

   ____

2. *¿Cómo está la mujer?* (How is the woman?)

   ____

3. *¿De dónde es la mujer?* (Where is the woman from?)
   a. Escocia   b. España   c. Egipto   d. Grecia

4. *¿De dónde es el hombre?* (Where is the man from?)
   a. Inglaterra   b. Australia   c. Irlanda   d. Italia

Writing:

Exercise 1.2.4

Write down where you and someone you know are from following the examples:

- Soy de Venezuela y él es de Chile.
- Ella es de España y tú eres de Inglaterra.
- Somos de Argentina.

1. ____

2. ____

Additional Vocabulary:

Below, you'll find some additional names of countries in Spanish. Pay attention to how they're pronounced! Just because they are spelled the same as (or similarly to) how they are in English, that doesn't necessarily mean they're said the same.

> **Note:** Again, these are not words you need to memorize right now. But they may come in handy one day, so make a note of them.

Listen to Track 1.2.11

- ***Argentina*** – Argentina
- ***Bolivia*** – Bolivia
- ***Chile*** – Chile
- ***Costa Rica*** – Costa Rica
- ***Croacia*** – Croatia
- ***Cuba*** – Cuba
- ***Dinamarca*** – Denmark
- ***La República Dominicana*** – The Dominican Republic
- ***El Salvador*** – El Salvador
- ***Ecuador*** – Ecuador
- ***Guatemala*** – Guatemala
- ***Filipinas*** – Philippines
- ***Honduras*** – Honduras
- ***Hungría*** – Hungary
- ***Jamaica*** – Jamaica
- ***Letonia*** – Latvia
- ***Lituania*** – Lithuania
- ***Nicaragua*** – Nicaragua
- ***Noruega*** – Norway
- ***Marruecos*** – Morocco
- ***Panamá*** – Panama
- ***Paraguay*** – Paraguay
- ***Perú*** – Peru
- ***Puerto Rico*** – Puerto Rico
- ***República Checa*** – Czech Republic
- ***Rumanía*** – Romania
- ***Suecia*** – Sweden
- ***Suiza*** – Switzerland
- ***Uruguay*** – Uruguay
- ***Venezuela*** – Venezuela

A Quick Recap of this Lesson

- In this chapter we talked about spelling.
- We also looked at how to ask, *"¿De dónde eres?" or "¿De dónde es?"*
- We learned how to answer the question: *"Soy de…"*

ANSWERS:

Exercise 1.2.1

1. U I E O A
2. E A U I O
3. E-S-P-A-Ñ-O-L (Spanish), T-R-A-B-A-J-O (Work/Job), D-I-N-E-R-O (Money)

Exercise 1.2.2

1. S-U-D-A-F-R-I-C-A 2. P-O-R-T-U-G-A-L 3. E-S-C-O-C-I-A
4. B-E-L-G-I-C-A 5. E-S-P-A-Ñ-A

Exercise 1.2.3

1. Joaquín 2. Muy bien 3. Ireland / Irlanda 4. Egypt / Egipto

Transcript:

Hombre: Buenos días. (Good day.)
Mujer: Hola. (Hello.)

Hombre: Cómo te llamas? (What is your name?)
Mujer: Me llamo Alejandra. ¿Cómo te llamas? (My name is Alejandra. What is your name?)

Hombre: Me llamo Joaquín. (My name is Joaquín.)
Mujer: ¿Joaquín? (Joaquín?)

Hombre: Sí. J-O-A-Q-U-I-N. Joaquín. (Yes. J-O-A-Q-U-I-N. Joaquín.)
Mujer: Y ¿Cómo estás, Joaquín? (And how are you, Joaquín?)

Hombre: Estoy así-así. ¿Y tú? ¿Cómo estás? (I'm so-so. And you? How are you?)
Mujer: Yo estoy muy bien. (I am very well.)

Hombre: ¿De dónde eres, Alejandra? (Where are you from, Alejandra?)
Mujer: Yo soy de Egipto. ¿Y tú? ¿De dónde eres? (I am from Egypt. And you? Where are you from?)

Hombre: Yo soy de Irlanda. (I am from Ireland.)

Week 1, Day 3: Spanish Pronunciation and Counting

What's in store for you today: Pronunciation and Counting

> **Today's goals are:**
>
> - To learn about and understand Spanish pronunciation
> - To learn to count to 20

Listen to Track 1.3.1

María: *Buenas tardes. Yo soy María Estévez.* (Good afternoon. I am María Estévez.)

Juan: *¿Estévez? ¿Cómo se escribe?* (Estévez? How is that written?)

María: *E-S-T-E-V-E-Z.* (E-S-T-E-V-E-Z.)

Juan: *Ah, muy bien. Hola, María. Yo soy Juan García.* (Oh, very good. Hello, María. I am Juan García.)

Maria: *Hola, Juan. ¿De dónde es?* (Hello, Juan. Where are you from?)

Juan: *Yo soy de Argentina. ¿Y usted?* (I am from Argentina. And you?)

María: *Yo soy de España.* (I am from Spain.)

Juan: *¿Cuál es su número de teléfono, María?* (What is your phone number, María?)

María: *Mi número de teléfono es Seis-Seis-Cuatro Nueve-Ocho-Cero-Siete* (My phone number is six-six-four nine-eight-zero-seven.)

How the Letters Sound

Now that we know the alphabet, let's take those letters spd actually put them into words and see what they sound like! First, let's look at the vowels. Below you'll find all the vowel sounds and vowel combinations you'll ever need to know in Spanish!

Listen to Track 1.3.2

Vowel (Vowel combination)	How it sounds	Example Word	Meaning of Example Word
A	"Ah"	Araña	Spider
E	"Eh"	Elefante	Elephant
I	"Ee"	Isla	Island
O	"Oh"	Oso	Bear
U	"Oo"	Uvas	Grapes
Ai*	"Ay"	Bailar	To dance
Ay*	"Ay"	Hay	There is/There are
Au*	"Ow"	Aunque	Although
Ei*	"Ey"	Aceite	Oil
Ie*	"Yeh"	Bien	Well
Ue*	"Weh"	Cuello	Neck

*These vowel combinations are called diphthongs. Diphthongs are sounds made by two vowels that act as one syllable.

Listen to Track 1.3.3

Some of the consonants in Spanish make the same sounds as our consonants in English. They are:

B, D, F, L, M, N, S, T, W

The rest, though, will sound just a little bit different. Let's take a look at those now!

Listen to Track 1.3.4

Consonant	Pronunciation	Example Word	Meaning of Example Word
C* (before an "i" or an "e")	"S"	*Cena*	Dinner
C (before an "a," "o," or "u")	"K"	*Casa*	House

CC	"K" followed immediately by "S"	*Dirección*	Address
D (Between vowels)	"Th"	*Cada*	Every
G (Before an "a," "o," or "u")	"G"	*Ganar*	To win
G (Before an "i" or "e")	"H"	*Gente*	People
H	*Not Pronounced* (Always silent)	*Hola*	Hello
J	"H"	*Jamón*	Ham
LL	Pronounced like the "y" in "yellow"	*Llamar*	To call
Ñ	Pronounced like the "ny" in "canyon"	*Mañana*	Tomorrow
Qu	"K"	*Queso*	Cheese
R	*Rolled one time*	*Pero*	But
RR	*Rolled multiple times*	*Perro*	Dog
V	"B"	*Vale*	Okay
X	Pronounced like the "x" in "exit"	*Extranjero*	Foreigner
Y	"Y" unless by itself, then it's pronounced "ee"	*Ya/ Y*	Already/And
Z*	"S"	*Cebra*	Zebra

***Note:** In Spain, these two consonants would be pronounced differently. They would both be said like a "**th**."

Exercise 1.3.1

Listen to Track 1.3.5

Listen to the track once through, repeating the words as they're said. Then listen to the track again. The second time through, write the words out as you listen to them. See if you can spell them correctly!

- ______________________
- ______________________
- ______________________

- ______________________
- ______________________
- ______________________

Exercise 1.3.2

This time, look at the list of words before you listen to the track. See if you can figure out how to pronounce them. Listen to the track, and compare how you say them to how a native Spanish speaker does.

Listen to Track 1.3.6

- ***Béisbol*** – Baseball
- ***Biblioteca*** – Library

- ***Perro*** – Dog
- ***Pero*** – But

Now, listen to the track again, and repeat the words after the speaker says them. Try to imitate their pronunciation.

Accent Marks – are they really that important?

Yes. One hundred and ten percent yes – they are important. The accent marks let you know where the stress in the word falls (i.e. where you put the emphasis). Knowing where to put the stress is very important because sometimes it can change the meaning of a word.

Before we look at accent marks, though, let's talk about the words in Spanish that **don't** have them. Even though the accents (**or *tildes***) aren't written in, the words still have a place where the stress will fall.

Rules to Remember:

Listen to Track 1.3.7

- Words that end in a vowel, **n**, or **s** → the stress is on the penultimate (**next to last**) syllable.
  - *Todo* – All
  - *Examen* – Exam/Test
  - *Lunes* – Monday

- Words ending in a consonant (**not** *n* or *s*) → the stress falls on the last syllable.
  - *Animal* – Animal
  - *Profesor* – Professor/Teacher
  - *Feliz* – Happy

Exercise 1.3.3

Listen to Track 1.3.8

Decide where the stress falls in each of the following words. After you've decided where you think the stress should fall, listen to the track to see if you're right.

- *Perro – Perro*
- *Tienda – Tienda*
- *Mujer – Mujer*

- *Hombre – Hombre*
- *Hospital – Hospital*

Accent Marks – when we use them

If a word breaks one of these rules (i.e. the stress doesn't fall on the "correct" syllable according to what category it fits into), then an accent mark will be written over the vowel that will take the stress.

Note: ONLY vowels will take accents in Spanish.

Listen to Track 1.3.9

Here are some examples of words with accent marks. Don't forget to pay close attention to how they're being pronounced, and try to repeat them after the speaker says them.

- ***Árbol*** – Tree
- ***Música*** – Music
- ***Teléfono*** – Telephone
- ***Café*** – Coffee OR Café

¡Uno, Dos, y Tres!

Listen to Track 1.3.10

We've talked a lot about letters lately. Let's mix it up a little and throw in some numbers! Here's how you count to 20 in Spanish. As you listen to the track, pay very close attention to how they're being pronounced and try to imitate the pronunciation.

- ***Cero*** – Zero
- ***Uno*** – One
- ***Dos*** – Two
- ***Tres*** – Three
- ***Cuatro*** – Four
- ***Cinco*** – Five
- ***Seis*** – Six
- ***Siete*** – Seven
- ***Ocho*** – Eight
- ***Nueve*** – Nine
- ***Diez*** – Ten
- ***Once*** – Eleven
- ***Doce*** – Twelve
- ***Trece*** – Thirteen
- ***Catorce*** – Fourteen
- ***Quince*** – Fifteen
- ***Dieciséis*** – Sixteen
- ***Diecisiete*** – Seventeen
- ***Dieciocho*** – Eighteen
- ***Diecinueve*** – Nineteen
- ***Veinte*** – Twenty

Exercise 1.3.4

Pop quiz! How many of the numbers above have a diphthong? _______________

Exercise 1.3.5

Listen to Track 1.3.11

Listen as the speaker reads thrcc lists of numbers. Write them down as you hear them:

- __ __ __ __ __
- __ __ __ __ __
- __ __ __ __ __
- __ __ __ __ __

Practice Corner

Listening and Vocabulary

Exercise 1.3.6

Listen to Track 1.3.12

Listen as Juan answers the question, *"¿Cuál es tu número de teléfono?"* and answer the question:

- What is Juan's phone number? _______________________________________

Pronunciation:

Listen to Track 1.3.13

Look at the words below. How are they pronounced? Where does the stress fall? See if you can say them correctly, then listen to the track and compare.

- *Correo* – Mail
- *Huevo* – Egg
- *Junio* – June
- *Todo* – All
- *Girasol* – Sunflower
- *Ganar* – To win

Stress:

- *Correo* (e+o is *not* a diphthong. This means that the "o" here is a syllable of its own.)
- *Huevo*
- *Junio*
- *Todo*
- *Girasol*
- *Ganar*

Writing:

Exercise 1.3.7

Write out your phone number, spelling out the letters in Spanish.

- *Mi número de teléfono es* (My phone number is):

____

A Quick Recap of this Lesson

Today we talked about:

- Pronunciation in Spanish.
- <u>Diphthongs</u> like "ie," "ai," and "ue." And we mentioned that a diphthong will make up one syllable.
- Accents and where stress falls in words:
  - Words that end in a vowel, *n*, or *s* → the stress is on the penultimate (next to last) syllable.
    - *Todo* – All
    - *Examen* – Exam/Test
    - *Lunes* – Monday
  - Words ending in a consonant (**not** *n* or *s*) → the stress falls on the last syllable
    - *Animal* – Animal
    - *Profesor* – Professor/Teacher
    - *Feliz* – Happy
  - And accent marks are used when the stress <u>doesn't</u> fall where it "should."
  - How to count to 20.

ANSWERS:

Exercise 1.3.1:

Hola, Gracias, Encantado, Aceite, Extranjero, Aunque

Exercise 1.3.3:

Perro, Tienda, Mujer, Hombre, Hospital

Exercise 1.3.4:

Ten (10)

Exercise 1.3.5:

- Cinco-Dos-Tres-Nueve-Siete: **5-2-3-9-7**
- Quince-Diez-Dieciocho-Cuatro-Cero: **15-10-18-4-0**
- Trece-Catorce-Doce-Dos-Tres: **13-14-12-2-3**
- Seis-Dieciséis-Siete-Diecisiete-Veinte: **6-16-7-17-20**

Exercise 1.3.6:

525-7934

Transcript:

María: ¿Cuál es tu número de teléfono?
Juan: Mi número de teléfono es: Cinco-Dos-Cinco Siete-Nueve-Tres-Cuatro

Week 1, Day 4: Counting to 99

What's in store for you today: Counting to 99

- To learn to count to 99
- To learn some basic vocabulary

Listen to Track 1.4.1

Juan: _Necesito un lápiz ¿Tienes un lápiz?_ (I need a pencil. Do you have a pencil?)

María: _No, lo siento. Tengo un bolígrafo._ (No, I'm sorry. I have a pen.)

Juan: _También necesito papel y una goma._ (I need paper and an eraser, too.)

María: _¿Algo más?_ (Anything else?)

Juan: _No. Gracias._ (No. Thank you.)

Los números 20–99

Yesterday, we looked at how to count to 20. Some would say that those numbers are the hardest. Moving forward, it's really not that bad! Let's take a look.

Listen to Track 1.4.2

- _**Veintiuno**_ – Twenty-one
- _**Veintidós**_ – Twenty-two
- _**Veintitrés**_ – Twenty-three
- _**Veinticuatro**_ – Twenty-four
- _**Veinticinco**_ – Twenty-five
- _**Veintiséis**_ – Twenty-six
- _**Veintisiete**_ – Twenty-seven
- _**Veintiocho**_ – Twenty-eight
- _**Veintinueve**_ – Twenty-nine
- _**Treinta**_ – Thirty
- _**Treinta y cinco**_ – Thirty-five
- _**Cuarenta**_ – Forty
- _**Cuarenta y cinco**_ – Forty-five
- _**Cincuenta**_ – Fifty
- _**Cincuenta y cinco**_ – Fifty-five
- _**Sesenta**_ – Sixty

- ***Sesenta y cinco*** – Sixty-five
- ***Setenta*** – Seventy
- ***Setenta y cinco*** – Seventy-five
- ***Ochenta*** – Eighty
- ***Ochenta y cinco*** – Eighty-five
- ***Noventa*** – Ninety
- ***Noventa y cinco*** – Ninety-five

For the numbers past 20, you're basically going to say **"thirty and one"** (***treinta y uno***) or **"forty and six"** (***cuarenta y seis***).

The only ones that are a little different are the 20s, which will mush together to make one word. The challenge with these is more in the spelling than anything.

Exercise 1.4.1

Listen to Track 1.4.3

Listen to the numbers and write them down:

- ______ - ______ - ______ - ______
- ______ - ______ - ______ - ______
- ______ - ______ - ______ - ______

Vocabulary: Useful Words

Listen to Track 1.4.4

María está hablando de lo que necesita en su trabajo.

(María is talking about what she needs in her job.)

En mi trabajo, necesito un lápiz, un bolígrafo, papel y un ordenador portátil. No necesito un libro. Pero necesito un escritorio y una silla.

(In my job, I need a pencil, a pen, paper, and a laptop. I don't need a book. But I need a desk and a chair.)

Let's take some time to look at some new vocabulary. Specifically, let's look at some vocabulary you'll probably use every day (you can even use a lot of these words right now, I bet!).

As you listen to the words, focus on the pronunciation and where the stress falls in the words.

<u>*Listen to Track 1.4.5*</u>

La Oficina – The Office

- ***Lápiz*** – Pencil
- ***Bolígrafo*** – Pen
- ***Papel*** – Paper
- ***Goma (de borrar)**** – Eraser
- ***Escritorio*** – Desk

- ***Computadora*** – Computer
- ***Portátil*** – Laptop
- ***Libro*** – Book
- ***Silla*** – Chair
- ***Trabajo*** – Work/Job

* Literally translated, "***Goma de borrar***" means "**rubber of erasing**." You can call an eraser a "***goma de borrar***," a "***goma***," or a "***borrador***."

<u>*Listen to Track 1.4.6*</u>

Verbos – Verbs

- ***Estudiar*** – To study
- ***Trabajar*** – To work
- ***Comer*** – To eat

- ***Comprar*** – To buy
- ***Leer*** – To read

Exercise 1.4.2

<u>*Listen to Track 1.4.7*</u>

What do you need in order to do the following things?

Para escribir una carta (in order to write a letter)	*Para escribir un correo electrónico* (in order to write an email)	*Para leer* (in order to read)	*Para estudiar español* (in order to study Spanish)

Necesito...

Listen to Track 1.4.8

All of the words we just looked at can be used with the verb ***necesitar*** (**to need**).

- ***Necesito un lápiz.*** – I need a pencil.
- ***Necesito papel.*** – I need paper.
- ***Necesito estudiar.*** – I need to study.

Like in English, verbs in Spanish change depending on what subject they are associated with (**I need; he needs**...). This is called "**conjugating**."

We will look at conjugating more in detail later on. For now, let's focus on using the verb ***necesitar*** in the first person singular:

- ***Yo necesito*** (**I need**)

If we want to say "**I need two**..." we simply make the nouns we just learned plural. Making nouns plural in Spanish is very easy.

Rules to Remember:

Listen to Track 1.4.9

To make a noun plural, simply:

- **Add an -s to word**s ending in vowels.
  - ***Libro-Libros*** (book–books)

- **Add -es to words ending in consonants.**
  - ***Papel-Papeles*** (paper–papers)

- **If a word ends in -z, change the -z to a -c before adding the -es.**
  - ***Lápiz- Lápices*** (pencil–pencils)

Exercise 1.4.3

Listen to Track 1.4.10

Listen to the track and fill in the blanks:

Necesito _______________. Para _______________, necesito dos _______________, papel, y tres _______________. También, necesito un _______________.

Practice Corner

Listening:

Exercise 1.4.4

Listen to Track 1.4.11

Listen to the track and put these sentences in order:

- *necesito---una---nueva---computadora---comprar* - _______________________
- *en---- sillas---- necesito--- mi--- cuatro---oficina* - _______________________
- *este--- leer--- año--- necesito--- libros--- seis* - _______________________

Vocabulary and Writing:

Exercise 1.4.5

Write out the following items in Spanish (even the numbers):

- Fifty computers - _______________________________
- Seventy-eight pencils and sixty-seven pens - _______________________________________
- Twenty-four laptops - _______________________________
- Forty-six desks - _______________________________
- Thirty-eight chairs - _______________________________

Exercise 1.4.6

Look around your desk (or table, or wherever you are right now). Write out how many of the following things you see:

Example: *En mi oficina, hay...* (In my office, there are ...)

- *Lápices* (Pencils)
- *Bolígrafos* (Pens)
- *Gomas* (Gums)
- *Sillas* (Chairs)
- *Libros* (Books)

____

____

____

____

Grammar and Vocabulary:

Exercise 1.4.7

Listen to the track and fill in the blanks:

Necesito _______________. Para _____________, necesito dos _____________, papel y tres _______. También, necesito un _____________. (I need to work. In order to work, I need two pens, paper, and three books. Also, I need a laptop.)

A Quick Recap of this Lesson

Today, we looked at:

- Counting from 20–99
- Basic vocabulary for the things around you
- And some vocabulary to express a few things you "need" to do
- We learned the verb **necesitar** (to need).

ANSWERS:

Exercise 1.4.1:

- Veintidós--cuarenta y tres--sesenta--ochenta y ocho: **22-43-60-88**
- Treinta y nueve--cincuenta y siete--noventa--veinticinco: **39-57-90-25**
- Setenta y seis--cuarenta--sesenta y uno—veintinueve: **76-40-61-29**

Exercise 1.4.2

Para escribir una carta (in order to write a letter)	Para escribir un correo electrónico (in order to write an email)	Para leer (in order to read)	Para estudiar español (in order to study Spanish)
Papel, bolígrafo, lápiz y goma. (Paper, pen, pencil and eraser)	Portátil, computador, escritorio, silla. (Laptop, computer, desk, chair.)	Libro, silla. (Book, chair.)	Libro, computadora, lápiz, bolígrafo, papel, silla, escritorio. (Book, computer, pencil, pen, paper, chair, desk.)

Exercise 1.4.3

Necesito trabajar. Para trabajar, necesito dos bolígrafos, papel y tres libros. También, necesito un portátil. (I need to work. In order to work, I need two pens, paper, and three books. Also, I need a laptop.)

Exercise 1.4.4

Necesito comprar una computadora nueva. (I need to buy a new laptop.)

Necesito cuatro sillas en mi oficina. (I need four chairs in my office.)

Necesito leer seis libros este año. (I need to read six books this year.)

Exercise 1.4.5

- Cincuenta computadoras
- Setenta y ocho lápices y sesenta y siete bolígrafos
- Veinticuatro portátiles
- Cuarenta y seis escritorios
- Treinta y ocho sillas

Exercise 1.4.6

- En mi escritorio, hay...
- Cero lápices (Zero pencils)
- Dos bolígrafos (Two pens)
- Tres gomas (Three rubbers)
- Cuatro sillas (Four chairs)
- Veintinueve libros (Twenty-nine books)

Exercise 1.4.7

Necesito trabajar. Para trabajar, necesito dos bolígrafos, papel y tres libros. También, necesito un portátil.

Week 1, Day 5: Nouns

What's in store for you today: Nouns

Listen to Track 1.5.1

María: *Bienvenido a mi casa.* (Welcome to my house.)

Juan: *Gracias.* (Thank you.)

María: *Vamos al salón. Allí tengo unas silla y la televisión. Podemos ver algo. La comida está en la cocina. Todavía está en el horno.* (Let's go to the living room. There, I have chairs and the television. We can watch something. The food is in the kitchen. It's still in the oven.)

Juan: *¿Dónde está el baño?* (Where is the bathroom?)

María: *Uno está aquí, y el otro está cerca del salón. Hay dos baños en mi casa.* (One is here, and the other is close to the living room. There are two bathrooms in my house.)

Noun Genders

WHAT?! Nouns have a gender? Yes, as a matter of fact they do. In Spanish, at least.

Listen to Track 1.5.2

- ***Mesa*** – Table (feminine)
- ***Perro*** – Dog (masculine)
- ***Libro*** – Book (masculine)
- ***Casa*** – House (feminine)

Rules to Remember:

Listen to Track 1.5.3

- Generally speaking, words that end in **-o** are masculine (***perro/libro***).
- and words that end in **-a** are feminine (***mesa/ casa***).

Seems simple enough! But be careful, because there are nouns that don't end in **-o** or **-a**. What about those?

Listen to Track 1.5.4

- ***Mujer*** – Woman (feminine)
- ***Hombre*** – Man (masculine)
- ***Árbol*** – Tree (masculine)
- ***Lección*** – Lesson (feminine)

It may seem a little overwhelming now, but getting used to identifying if a noun is masculine or feminine early on will make your Spanish-learning journey that much easier. So, to get you started, below you will find a few handy rules to remember when trying to figure out the gender of a noun.

Masculine	Feminine
• Ends in *-o* • Ends in an accented vowel (á, é, í, ó, ú) • Ends in *-ma* (be careful with this one!) • Ends in a consonant that isn't *-d* or *-z* • Ends in *-e*	• Ends in *-a* • Ends in *-sión* or *-ción* • Ends in *-dad* or *-tad* or *-tud* • Ends in *-umbre* • Ends in *-d* or *-z*

It isn't completely necessary right now to memorize all of these rules. It is important, however, that you become aware of this concept and understand it. It's good to get some practice with it, as well. So that's what we'll do.

Exercise 1.5.1

Now that we know the rules for determining when a word is masculine or feminine, let's see how well we can put what we've talked about into practice.

Decide which of these nouns are masculine and which are feminine (some of them will be new to you):

Listen to Track 1.5.5

1. ***Amigo**** – Friend
2. ***Niño**** – Child
3. ***Biblioteca*** – Library
4. ***Tienda*** – Store
5. ***Ciudad*** – City
6. ***Parque*** – Park
7. ***Papel*** – Paper
8. ***Escuela*** – School
9. ***Bolígrafo*** – Pen
10. ***País*** – Country
11. ***Mundo*** – World
12. ***Persona***** – Person

Masculine Nouns	Feminine Nouns

*These two nouns can change gender based on who you're talking about: "my female friend" would be "***mi amiga***." "The little girl" would be "***la niña***."

This word does not change based on who you're talking about. Even if the person you're talking about is a man, he is still a "*persona***."

¡Ojo! (Look out!)

Listen to Track 1.5.6

> **Note:** As you will discover as we go along, there are ALWAYS exceptions in Spanish.
>
> For example, ***día*** ("day") ends in an -*a* but is, in fact, masculine. And ***lápiz*** ("pencil") ends in "-*z*" but is masculine as well!

What's in Your Home/ *En mi casa...*

Now that we know how to identify if a noun is masculine or feminine, we need some nouns that we can work with! For today's vocabulary section, let's talk about "in my house..."

Listen to Track 1.5.7

- ***Casa*** – House
- ***Salón*** – Living room
- ***Baño*** – Bathroom
- ***Cocina*** – Kitchen
- ***Habitación*** – Bedroom
- ***Cama*** – Bed
- ***Puerta*** – Door
- ***Ventana*** – Window
- ***Pared*** – Wall
- ***Sofá**** – Couch/Sofa
- ***Lámpara*** – Lamp

- ***Televisión*** – Television
- ***Silla*** – Chair
- ***Nevera*** – Refrigerator
- ***Horno*** – Oven
- ***Estufa*** – Stove
- ***Microondas**** – Microwave
- ***Inodoro*** – Toilet
- ***Ducha*** – Shower
- ***Bañera*** – Bathtub
- ***Oficina*** – Office

* ***Sofá*** is irregular (it's masculine).

** ***Microondas*** is singular AND masculine – it's doubly irregular!

Exercise 1.5.2

Let's try to put the words we just learned into our "masculine" or "feminine" categories:

Masculine Nouns	Feminine Nouns

What's in your home?

Exercise 1.5.3

Listen to Track 1.5.8

Listen to the track and fill in the blanks:

Juan está hablando de su casa. (Juan is talking about his house.)

*En mi casa hay (there is/there are) _____________ habitaciones y dos ___________.
Hay un ___________, y una _____________. En el _____________, hay cuatro
_____________ y una _____________. Hay tres ___________ y seis _____________.*

A few things to note:

Listen to Track 1.5.9

You might have noticed a few things about the last recording. For example,
habitaciones doesn't have an accent.

- When making words that end in **-ción** plural, you add an *-es* and drop the
  accent mark.

We saw the word **hay**. This means "there is/there are" and is very handy!

Also, when we were talking about "one bathroom" the number one (**uno**) became
un and for "one kitchen" it became **una**.

- When we want to say "*one something*" (i.e. the "one" is an adjective saying
  how many of something there is), it will become:
  o **Un** with masculine objects and
  o **Una** with feminine objects

Practice Corner

Listening:

Exercise 1.5.4

Listen to Track 1.5.10

Listen to the dialogue and answer the questions:

Juan tiene una casa nueva. Está hablando con María sobre su casa.
(Juan has a new house. He's talking with María about his house.)

1. *¿Cuántas habitaciones hay en la casa de Juan?* (How many rooms are in Juan's house?) - _______________________________

2. *¿Cuántas camas hay en la casa de Juan?* (How many beds are in Juan's house?) - _______________________________

3. *¿Cuántos baños hay en su casa?* (How many bathrooms are in your home?) - _______________________________

4. *¿Qué NO tiene el salón de Juan?* (What does NOT have Juan's room?)
   a. *Una television* (a television)   c. *Sillas* (chairs)
   b. *Un sofá* (a sofa)   d. *Lámparas* (lamps)

Writing and Vocabulary:

Exercise 1.5.5

Write a few sentences about your house.

____

____

____

Grammar:

Exercise 1.5.6

These nouns have been divided up into groups of Masculine Nouns and Feminine Nouns. But there are some mistakes! Five of these nouns are in the wrong category. Can you figure out which ones?

Masculine Nouns	Feminine Nouns
• *Perro*	• *Puerta*
• *Libro*	• *Sofá*
• *Lápiz*	• *Televisión*
• *Ciudad*	• *Papel*
• *Hombre*	• *Lámpara*
• *Hospital*	• *Pared*
• *Portátil*	• *Bolígrafo*
• *Silla*	• *Nevera*

A Quick Recap of this Lesson

Today, we worked to become familiar with nouns in Spanish. We...

- Talked about the difference between masculine and feminine nouns.

We also looked at vocabulary for items around your house and learned how to say things such as, "***hay dos baños en mi casa***" (There are two bathrooms in my house.)

ANSWERS:

Exercise 1.5.1

Masculine Nouns	Feminine Nouns
Amigo, Niño, Parque, Papel, Bolígrafo, País, Mundo	Biblioteca, Tienda, Ciudad, Escuela, Persona, (Amiga), (Niña),

Exercise 1.5.2

Masculine Nouns	Feminine Nouns
Sofá, Inodoro, Horno, Salón, Baño, Microondas,	Casa, Puerta, Ventana, Lámpara, Ducha, Bañera, Nevera, Estufa, Cama, Silla, Televisión, Cocina, Habitación,

Exercise 1.5.3

En mi casa hay dos habitaciones y dos camas. Hay un baño y una cocina. En el salón, hay cuatro lámparas y una televisión. Hay tres puertas y seis ventanas.

(In my house, there are two bedrooms and two beds. There is one bathroom and one kitchen. In the living room, there are four lamps and one television. There are three doors and six windows.)

Exercise 1.5.4

1. tres habitaciones / three bedrooms
2. dos camas/two beds

3. tres baños/three bathrooms
4. Un sofá/Sofa

Transcript:

María: ¿Cuántas habitaciones hay en tu casa? (How many bedrooms are there in your house?)

Juan: Hay tres habitaciones en mi casa. Tres habitaciones y dos camas. Una habitación es una oficina. (There are three bedrooms in my house. Three bedrooms and two beds. One bedroom is an office.)

María: Y, ¿cuántos baños hay? (And, how many bathrooms are there?)

Juan: Hay tres baños, también. (There are three bathrooms, too.)

María: Y en el salón, ¿qué hay? (And in the living room, what is there?)

Juan: Hay una televisión y cuatro sillas. También hay dos lámparas. (There is one television and four chairs. Also, there are two lamps.)

María: No hay un sofá? (There isn't a sofa?)

Juan: No, no hay un sofá. (No, there isn't a sofa.)

Exercise 1.5.5

- Una habitación, un baño, una cocina y un salón (A room, a bathroom, a kitchen and a living room)
- Una nevera, un horno, una estufa, una mesa, y dos sillas (A fridge, an oven, a stove, a table, and two chairs)
- Un inodoro y una ducha (A toilet and a shower)
- Un sofá, dos sillas, dos lámparas y una televisión (A sofa, two chairs, two lamps and a televisión)

Exercise 1.5.6:

Ciudad, Silla, Sofá, Papel, Bolígrafo

Week 1 Recap

This last week, we have looked at introducing ourselves, spelling, pronunciation, and some basic vocabulary. Let's take some time to review everything before we move on to Week 2.

Listening:

Listen to Track WR 1.1

Exercise WR 1.1

Listen to the track and answer the questions:

1. *¿Cómo se llama el hombre?* (What is the name of man?) - ________________
2. *¿Cómo se llama la mujer?* (What is the woman's name?) - ________________
3. *¿De dónde es la mujer?* (Where is the woman from?) - ________________
4. *¿De dónde es el hombre?* (Where is the man from?) - ________________

Listen to Track WR 1.2

Exercise WR 1.2

Listen to the track and fill in the blanks:

Hombre: *Hola, Lucía.*

Mujer: *Hola, Marco. ¿Qué tal?*

Hombre: ________________. *Hace mucho que no te veo.*

Mujer: *Sí. Hace mucho.*

Hombre: *¿* ________________ *?*

Mujer: *Yo estoy* ____________.

Hombre: *Muy bien. Pues me tengo que ir. ¿Te llamo algún día?*

Mujer: *Sí. Mi número de teléfono es:* ________________________________.

Hombre: *¿Me lo repites?*

Mujer: *Sí. Mi número de teléfono es:* ____________ *cuarenta y nueve veintidós.*

Hombre: *Gracias.* __________________.

Mujer: ________________.

Listen to Track WR 1.3

Exercise WR 1.3

Listen as the speaker spells out some words. Try to write them down as you hear them. What do they say?

- ___-___-___-___
- ___-___-___-___-___-___
- ___-___-___-___-___-___-___-___-___-___
- ___-___-___-___-___-___-___

Writing:

Exercise WR 1.4

Write out a dialogue between Sara and Jorge. Have them introduce themselves, and ask a few simple "getting to know you" questions.

For a sample, see the dialogue in Listening part 1.

____

____

____

____

Exercise WR 1.5

Look around your desk right now. Write out what you see:

Example:

En mi escritorio, hay un portátil, dos bolígrafos y tres lápices. No hay gomas. No hay una computadora. Hay una silla. Hay cuatro libros. (On my desk are a laptop, two pens, and three pencils. There are no erasers. There is no computer. There's a chair. There are four books)

____

____

____.

Vocabulary:

Exercise WR 1.6

Parts of these sentences don't make sense. Correct them so that they do:

- *En mi cocina, hay un microondas, una nevera, un horno y una ducha.*

  ____

- *En mi baño, hay una cama, un inodoro y una bañera.*

  ____

- *En mi salón, hay una televisión, un sofá y dos lámparas. También, hay tres neveras y dos ventanas.*

  ____

Exercise WR 1.7

Translate the sentences below:

- *En mi cocina, hay un microondas, una nevera, un horno y una estufa.*

  ____

- *En mi baño, hay una ducha, un inodoro y una bañera.*

  ____

- *En mi salón, hay una televisión, un sofá y dos lámparas. También, hay tres sillas y dos ventanas.*

  ____

Grammar:

Exercise WR 1.8

Which of these words are feminine and which are masculine?

- **Perro** – Dog
- **Libro** – Book
- **Mesa** – Desk
- **Nevera** – Fridge
- **Sofá** – Sofa/Couch
- **Escritorio** – Desk
- **Puerta** – Door
- **Huevo** – Egg
- **Portátil** – Laptop
- **Ducha** – Shower
- **Persona** – Person
- **Tienda** – Store
- **Baño** – Bathroom

Masculine	Feminine

Listen to Track WR 1.4

Exercise WR 1.9

1. Listen to the track and decide:
2. Are they being formal or informal? ____________________________
   a. Which of these phrases would go in the blank?
   b. Es un placer conocerle
3. What phrase could they use to say, "farewell?"
   a. Buenas
   b. Buenas tardes
   c. Nos vemos
   d. Hola

ANSWERS:

Exercise WR 1.1:

1. Ricardo García
2. Ana González
3. México
4. Miami, Estados Unidos

Transcript :

Hombre: Buenos días. (Good day.)

Mujer: Hola. Buenos días. (Hello. Good day.)

Hombre: Yo soy Ricardo García. ¿Cómo se llama usted? (I am Ricardo García. What is your name?)

Mujer: Me llamo Ana González (My name is Ana Gonzalez.)

Hombre: Es un placer conocerle. (It's a pleasure to meet you.)

Mujer: Igualmente. (The same to you.)

Hombre: ¿De dónde es, Ana? (Where are you from, Ana?)

Mujer: Yo soy de México. Y usted, ¿de dónde es? (I am from Mexico. And you, where are you from?)

Hombre: Yo soy de Miami, en los Estados Unidos. (I am from Miami, in the United States.)

Exercise WR 1.2:

Hombre: Hola, Lucía. (Hello, Lucía.)

Mujer: Hola, Marco. ¿Qué tal? (Hello, Marco. How's it going?)

Hombre: Bien. Hace mucho que no te veo. (Good. It's been a long time since I've seen you.)

Mujer: Sí. Hace mucho. (Yes. A long time.)

Hombre: ¿Cómo estás? (How are you?)

Mujer: Yo estoy bien. (I'm well.)

Hombre: Muy bien. Pues me tengo que ir. ¿Te llamo algún día? (Very good. Well, I have to go. Can I call you some day?)

Mujer: Sí. Mi número de teléfono es: seis-seis-ocho cuarenta y nueve veintidos. (Yes. my phone number is: six-six-eight forty-nine twenty-two.)

Hombre: ¿Me lo repites? (Can you repeat it for me?)

Mujer: Sí. Mi número de teléfono es: seis-seis-ocho cuarenta y nueve veintidos. (Yes. My number is six-six-eight forty-nine twenty-two.)

Hombre: Gracias. Hasta luego. (Thank you, until later.)

Mujer: Hasta pronto. (See you soon!)

Exercise WR 1.3:

Gato – Cat

Escritorio – Desk

Egipto – Egypt

Trabajar – To work

Exercise WR 1.4:

Sofía: Hola.¿Cómo estas? (Hello, how are you?)

Jorge: Hola, estoy bien, gracias. ¿Y usted? (Hello. I'm fine, and you?)

Sofía: Estoy bien, gracias. (I'm fine, thank you.)

Jorge: ¿Cómo se llama? (What is your name?)

Sofía: Me llamo Sofía. ¿Y tú?¿Cómo te llamas? (My name is Sofía . And you? What is your name?)

Jorge: Me llamo Jorge. (My name is Jorge.)

Sofía: Hasta luego, Jorge. (See you later, Jorge.)

Jorge: Adiós, Sofía. (Goodbye, Sofía.)

Exercise WR 1.5:

Sample:

En mi escritorio, hay un portátil, dos bolígrafos y tres lápices. No hay gomas. No hay una computadora. Hay una silla. Hay cuatro libros.

(On my desk are a laptop, two pens, and three pencils. There are no erasers. There is no computer. There's a chair. There are four books)

Exercise WR 1.6

- En mi cocina, hay un microondas, una nevera, un horno y una **estufa**. (In my kitchen, there is a microwave, refrigerator, oven, and stove.)
- En mi baño, hay una **ducha**, un inodoro y una bañera. (In my bathroom, there is a shower, a toilet and a bathtub.)
- En mi salón, hay una televisión, un sofá y dos lámparas. También, hay tres **sillas** y dos ventanas. (In my living room, there is a television, a sofa and two lamps. Also, there are three chairs and two windows.)

Exercise WR 1.7

- In my kitchen, there is a microwave, a refrigerator, an oven, and a stove.
- In my bathroom, there is a shower, a toilet, and a bathtub.
- In my living room, there is a television, a couch, and two lamps. Also, there are three chairs and two windows.

Exercise WR 1.8

Masculine	Feminine
Perro, Libro, Sofá, Escritorio, Huevo, Portátil, Baño	Mesa, Nevera, Puerta, Tienda, Ducha, Persona

Exercise WR 1.9

1. Informal
2. B (Es un placer conocerte [Nice to meet you].)
3. C (Nos vemos [*see ya*].)

Transcript:

Hombre: Hola, yo soy Héctor. ¿Cómo te llamas? (Hello, I am Héctor. What is your name?)

Mujer: Hola, Héctor. Yo soy María. (Hello, Héctor. I am María.)

Hombre: Encantado. (Pleased to meet you.)

Mujer: ________________________. (It's a pleasure to meet you.)

Week 2, Day 1: Definite and Indefinite Articles

What's in store for you today: Articles

- To learn how to use definite and indefinite articles
- To learn food vocabulary

Listen to Track 2.1.1

María: _Necesito ir de compras. Necesito comprar unas cosas._ (I need to go shopping. I need to buy some things.)

Juan: _¿Por qué?_ (Why?)

María: _Voy a hacer una cena para mi amiga._ (I am going to make dinner for my friend.)

Juan: _¿Qué vas a hacer?_ (What are you going to make?)

María: _Voy a hacer pollo con verduras. Tengo una receta nueva._ (I am going to make chicken with vegetables. I have a new recipe.)

Juan: _¿Qué necesitas en la tienda?_ (What do you need at the store?)

María: _Necesito las zanahorias, la cebolla y ajo. Tengo unas patatas en casa. Y para el postre necesito unas manzanas. ¡Voy a hacer un pastel de manzana!_ (I need the carrots and the onion and garlic. I have some potatoes at home. And for the dessert, I need some apples. I'm going to make an apple pie!)

Definite and Indefinite Articles

Last week, we talked about how nouns can be masculine or feminine. Sometimes, this can be a little confusing (especially at the beginning). So, one way to help yourself remember if a noun is masculine or feminine is to immediately learn an article with it!

Today, we're going to look at what the articles are in Spanish. But before we get too far ahead of ourselves, let's discuss what an article actually is.

In English...

- We have one definite article: *"the"*
- We have two indefinite articles which are: *"a/an"* and *"some"*

Definite Articles

Let's start with the Spanish equivalent of "the." Just like with nouns (which can be singular or plural, masculine or feminine), our articles can take on different forms. The form they take on will depend on <u>which noun they are defining</u>.

Listen to Track 2.1.2

El libro – The book

La mesa – The table

Los libros – The books

Las mesas – The tables

Rules to Remember:

Listen to Track 2.1.3

The definite articles in Spanish are:

- *El* (The) – is used with singular, masculine nouns.
- *La* (The) – is used with singular, feminine nouns.
- *Los* (The) – is used with plural, masculine nouns.
- *Las* (The) – is used with plural, feminine nouns.

Exercise 2.1.1

So how would you say the following?

1. The lamps
2. The bathroom
3. The pens
4. The chairs
5. The books
6. The desk
7. The oven
8. The refrigerator

Indefinite Articles

Just like definite articles, our indefinite articles have a few different forms they can take on. Again, what form they use will depend on the noun they are describing.

Listen to Track 2.1.4

Un libro – A book	***Unos libros*** – Some books
Una mesa – A table	***Unas mesas*** – Some tables

The indefinite articles in Spanish are:

- ***Un*** (A) – is used with singular, masculine nouns.
- ***Una*** (A) – is used with singular, feminine nouns.
- ***Unos*** (Some) – is used with plural, masculine nouns.
- ***Unas*** (Some) – is used with plural, feminine nouns.

Some of these may look familiar from when we were talking about how to say "one…" In Spanish, instead of saying "one pen" you will be saying "a pen" (***un bolígrafo***).

Exercise 2.1.2

How would you say the following?

1. A wall	5. An eraser
2. Some windows	6. Some paper
3. A pencil	7. A shower
4. Some bathrooms	8. Some beds

An extra note to remember:

Listen to Track 2.1.5

Resist the urge to use indefinite articles with uncountable nouns! In Spanish, indefinite articles are not used with uncountable nouns. In English, we can say things like, "I need <u>some</u> milk." BUT, "milk" is uncountable (i.e. we can't say, "I need two milks" unless we are ordering "two <u>glasses</u> of milk" - in which case, "glasses" is countable).

Here is how you can say "I need milk" without using an indefinite article with the uncountable noun:

- *Necesito la leche.* (I need the milk.)
- *Necesito leche.* (I need [some] milk.)
- *Necesito dos vasos de leche.* (I need two glasses of milk.)

¡Comida! (Food!)

Now that we know our definite and indefinite articles, whenever we learn new vocabulary, we'll introduce it using the <u>definite</u> article that would be associated with it. This way, you'll instantly know if it's masculine or feminine!

<u>Listen to Track 2.1.6</u>

¡Necesito comer! (I need to eat!)

- *La manzana* – The apple
- *La naranja* – The orange
- *Las uvas* – The grapes
- *El plátano* – The banana
- *El aguacate* – The avocado
- *El brócoli* – The broccoli
- *La zanahoria* – The carrot
- *La cebolla* – The onion
- *El ajo** – The garlic
- *La lechuga** – The lettuce
- *La patata* – The potato
- *El huevo* – The egg
- *El pollo** – The chicken
- *La carne de vaca** – The beef
- *La carne de cerdo** – The pork
- *El pavo** – The turkey
- *El jamón** – The ham
- *El queso** – The cheese
- *La leche** – The milk
- *El pan** – The bread
- *La mostaza** – The mustard
- *El ketchup** – The ketchup
- *La mayonesa** – The mayonnaise

* These nouns are **<u>uncountable</u>**: We wouldn't say, "**I need two turkeys**" (**unless, of course, we're talking about the animal, which you can count. But for the meat itself, you cannot**). This means if we want to say, "**I need some turkey**" in Spanish, we would simply say *necesito pavo* (i.e. "I need turkey.")

Exercise 2.1.3

Translate the following sentences from Spanish into English:

- *Necesito comprar leche, queso, pan, carne de vaca, pollo, cebolla, ajo y unas manzanas.*

____

- *En mi sándwich, yo quiero pavo, queso, lechuga y mostaza.*

____

- *Necesito la catsup y la mayonesa, por favor .*

____

Practice Corner

Listening:

Listen to Track 2.1.7

Exercise 2.1.4

Juan necesita ir de compras. ¿Qué necesita comprar? (Juan needs to go shopping. What does he need to buy?)

Juan necesita comprar (Juan needs to buy):

- ________________________
- ________________________
- ________________________
- ________________________
- ________________________

Grammar and Vocabulary:

Exercise 2.1.5

When we talked about food, we learned the vocabulary with their <u>definite articles</u>. Let's pair some of those items with their <u>indefinite articles</u>.

How would you say the following?

- Some oranges
- Some avocados
- An onion
- Some eggs
- A potato

Exercise 2.1.6

And, just as a quick refresher of the other vocabulary we learned today, how would you say the following? (Try to do this without looking back!)

- The potatoes
- The beef
- The bread
- The grapes
- The apples
- The chicken
- The pork

Writing:

Take a moment to write out your shopping list. This is something you can start doing every time you go shopping. It will help to make your new Spanish vocabulary a part of your everyday life, thus make it easier for you to remember!

Additional Vocabulary:

Listen to Track 2.1.8

Here are a few more words you might want to look at:

- ***Más comida*** – More food
- ***La fruta*** – The fruit
- ***Las fresas*** – The strawberries
- ***La pera*** – The pear
- ***Las verduras*** – The vegetables
- ***El tomate*** – The tomato
- ***El espárrago*** – The asparagus
- ***El apio*** – The celery
- ***Un vaso*** – A glass
  - ***De agua*** – Of water
- ***De leche*** – Of milk
- ***De limonada*** – Of lemonade
- ***Refresco*** – Soda pop
- ***Té*** – Tea
- ***Café*** – Coffee
- ***Vino*** – Wine
  - ***Una copa de vino*** – A glass of wine
- ***Cerveza*** – Beer

Listen to Track 2.1.9

Otras palabras útiles (Other useful words)

- ***Y*** – And
- ***Pero*** – But
- ***Cosa*** – Thing
- ***Por favor*** – Please
- ***También*** – Also

A Quick Recap of this Lesson

Today, we talked about indefinite and definite articles:

The definite articles in Spanish are:

- *El* (The) – is used with singular, masculine nouns.
- *La* (The) – is used with singular, feminine nouns.
- *Los* (The) – is used with plural, masculine nouns.
- *Las* (The) – is used with plural, feminine nouns.

The indefinite articles in Spanish are:

- *Un* (A) – is used with singular, masculine nouns.
- *Una* (A) – is used with singular, feminine nouns.
- *Unos* (Some) – is used with plural, masculine nouns.
- *Unas* (Some) – is used with plural, feminine nouns.

We also learned vocabulary for talking about food.

ANSWERS:

Exercise 2.1.1

1. Las lámparas / 2. El baño / 3. Los bolígrafos / 4. Las sillas / 5. Los libros / 6. El escritorio / 7. El horno / 8. La nevera

Exercise 2.1.2

1. Una pared / 2. Unas ventanas / 3. Un lápiz / 4. Unos baños / 5. Una goma (de borrar) or Un borrador / 6. Unos papeles / 7. Una ducha / 8. Unas camas

Exercise 2.1.3

- I need to buy milk, cheese, bread, beef, chicken, onion, garlic, and some apples.
- In my sandwich, I want turkey, cheese, lettuce, and mustard.
- I need the ketchup and the mayonnaise, please.

Exercise 2.1.4

Unas uvas, Un plátano, Unas zanahorias, Unos huevos, Jamón
(Some grapes, A banana, Some carrots, Some eggs, Ham)

Transcript:

Necesito ir de compras. Necesito comprar unas cosas. Necesito unas uvas y un plátano. También, necesito unas zanahorias y unos huevos. Finalmente, necesito jamón.

(I need to go shopping. I need to buy some things. I need some grapes and a banana. Also, I need some carrots and some eggs. Finally, I need [some] ham.)

Exercise 2.1.5

- Some oranges - Unas naranjas
- Some avocados - Unos aguacates
- An onion - Una cebolla
- Some eggs - Unos huevos
- A potato - Una patata

Exercise 2.1.6

- The potatoes - Las patatas
- The beef - La carne de vaca/carne de res
- The bread - El pan
- The grapes - Las uvas
- The apples - Las manzanas
- The chicken - El pollo
- The pork - La carne de cerdo

Week 2, Day 2: Adjectives

Listen to Track 2.2.1

Mi madre es alta. Yo soy baja. Mi hermano es bajo, también. Mi padre es divertido, pero mi hermana es aburrida. Yo soy divertida. Mi madre es inteligente. Tenemos una casa roja. Es una casa pequeña. También es una casa limpia.

(My mother is tall. I am short. My brother is short, too. My dad is fun, but my sister is boring. I am fun. My mother is smart. We have a red house. It is a small house. It's also a clean house.)

Nouns Recap

Listen to Track 2.2.2

So far, we've learned that nouns can be 1) singular or plural and 2) masculine or feminine – which is weird for English speakers to wrap their heads around.

Words that end in -o like **_tiempo_*** ("time" or "weather") and **_momento_** ("moment") are masculine, and words that end in -a like **_cosa_** ("thing") and **_hora_** ("hour" or "time") are feminine. Not all nouns end in -o or -a, though. We talked about how words that end in -e are masculine, like **_nombre_** (name), and words that end in -cion like **_educación_** (education) are feminine.

Tiempo refers to time when you're speaking of <u>"time" in general</u> (i.e. I don't have a lot of time). _Hora_ refers to <u>a specific time</u> (i.e. What time is it?). We will go into this in more detail in a future chapter, so don't fret too much about it right now.

We looked at these rules and more yesterday. Today, we're going to learn how to do more than just say the nouns. We're going to learn how to <u>describe </u>them.

Adjectives

Before we jump in with both feet, let's take a moment to make sure we know what it is we're jumping into – a big pool of adjectives!

What are adjectives, exactly? Well, they're the words we use when we want to describe our nouns. They answer the questions: What kind? How many? How much? Which one?

For example: Which girl are you talking about? I'm talking about the <u>smart</u> girl.

Here, "smart" is describing the girl (telling you which girl we're talking about). We could also say "the <u>tall</u> building" or "the <u>cute</u> dog." When we want to explain that we're talking about "the <u>red</u> book" or "the <u>scary</u> movie," we use adjectives!

Listen to Track 2.2.3

As I'm sure you can imagine, being able to use adjectives in Spanish is very important. How else would you describe "***la chica inteligente***" ("the smart girl) or "***el edificio alto***" ("the tall building")?

Listen carefully to the following list of 25 of the most common adjectives spoken in Spanish. Don't forget to pay attention to the pronunciation. Listen once through carefully, and then again, repeating the words as you hear them.

Listen to Track 2.2.4

1. ***Alto**** – Tall
2. ***Bajo**** – Short
3. ***Grande*** – Big
4. ***Pequeño**** – Small
5. ***Rico**** – Rich
6. ***Pobre*** – Poor
7. ***Feo**** – Ugly
8. ***Guapo**** – Attractive/Handsome
9. ***Lindo**** – Pretty
10. ***Inteligente*** – Smart/Intelligent
11. ***Tonto**** – Stupid
12. ***Caro**** – Expensive
13. ***Barato**** – Cheap
14. ***Feliz*** – Happy
15. ***Triste*** – Sad
16. ***Fuerte*** – Strong
17. ***Débil*** – Weak
18. ***Limpio**** – Clean
19. ***Sucio**** – Dirty
20. ***Delgado**** – Skinny
21. ***Gordo**** – Fat
22. ***Bueno**** – Good
23. ***Malo**** – Bad
24. ***Divertido**** – Fun
25. ***Aburrido**** – Boring

Listen to Track 2.2.5

And, of course, the colors:

1. *Rojo** – Red
2. *Azul* – Blue
3. *Verde* – Green
4. *Amarillo** – Yellow
5. *Anaranjado OR Naranja** – Orange
6. *Negro** – Black
7. *Blanco** – White
8. *Rosa* – Pink
9. *Marrón* – Brown
10. *Gris* – Gray

*In Latin America, "*anaranjado*" is used to refer to the color, while "*naranja*" refers to the fruit. In Spain, "*naranja*" is used for both the color and the fruit.

Now that we have a good, working list of common Spanish adjectives, let's start talking technicalities. There are a few important rules you need to remember when using these useful parts of speech in Spanish.

Rules to Remember

Listen to Track 2.2.6

- Adjectives, like nouns, can be <u>singular or plural</u>. This is something we don't do in English, so you're going to want to let it sink in for a second. If you are talking about a noun in the plural form, then you will use an adjective in the plural form.
  - *Grande-grandes* (Big)
  - *Rico-ricos* (Rich)
  - *Azul-azules* (Blue)

- Also like nouns in Spanish, adjectives can be either masculine or feminine. If you go back and look at the list we just went over, you'll notice a bunch of those adjectives have an asterisk (*) next to them. If that's the case, that means they will change when they are in their feminine form. The -*o* will change to an -*a*.
  - *Alto-alta* (Tall)
  - *Rojo-roja* (Red)
  - *Limpio-limpia* (Clean)

- Some adjectives have two forms (those that don't end in -o), while others have four (those that do end in -o). Look at the chart below:

Adjectives with Two Forms (Singular-Plural)	Adjectives with Four Forms (Singular Masculine- Singular Feminine- Plural Masculine- Plural Feminine)
Inteligente- Inteligentes (Smart/ Intelligent) ***Feliz- Felices*** (Happy) ***Fuerte- Fuertes*** (Strong) ***Triste- Tristes*** (Sad) *****Naranja-Naranjas*** (Orange) *****Rosa-Rosas*** (Pink)	***Gordo-Gorda-Gordos-Gordas*** (Fat) ***Barato-Barata-Baratos-Baratas*** (Cheap) ***Amarillo-Amarilla-Amarillos-Amarillas*** (Yellow) ***Bajo-Baja-Bajos-Bajas*** (Short)

* If the adjective (singular) ends in –z, the plural form will end in –ces.

** These two colors will never end in an -o. Their singular form always ends in -a, even if they're defining a masculine noun.

Note: "**Naranja**" is the word for "orange" the fruit in Spain and Latin America. In Spain, "**naranja**" is also the word for "orange" the color. In Latin America, the term "**anaranjado**" is used for "**orange**" the color.

- Adjectives go <u>after the noun</u>.
  - In English, we would say "**the red house**." But, in Spanish they say, "***la casa roja***" (literally translated as "**the house red**").

The most important thing to remember is **AGREE AGREE AGREE!** Your adjectives have to agree with the nouns in both **<u>gender and number</u>**.

Listen to Track 2.2.7

El libro rojo – The red book

Los libros rojos – The red books

La ciudad grande – The big city

Las ciudades grandes – The big cities

El perro grande – The big dog

Los perros grandes – The big dogs

Notice in the examples above that if there is only one thing (**book, city, dog**), the adjective is singular (**no -s**). But if there is more than one book, city, or dog, the adjective is plural (**yes -s**). Also, notice that "book" is masculine in Spanish, so its adjective remains masculine in both the singular (***rojo***) and the plural (***rojos***).

When the adjective doesn't end in -o (like with grande) it remains the same in both the masculine example (**with *perro***) and the feminine (with *ciudad*). It changes between singular (***grande***) and plural (***grandes***) but not masculine and feminine.

> **Note:** Making an adjective plural is the same as making an noun plural. Add an -s to a word that ends in a vowel (***rojo-rojos***) and an -es to a word that ends in a consonant (***azul-azules***).

Exercise 2.2.1

Correct the adjectives in the following statements so that they agree with the noun they are describing:

1. *La cocina limpio* - _______________________
2. *Las casas pequeño* - _______________________
3. *Las mujeres feliz* - _______________________
4. *Los edificios feo* - _______________________
5. *La comida caro* - _______________________
6. *Los bolígrafos azul.* - _______________________

The Immediate Family

Let's put some of these new words to good use. In order to do this, let's learn another small group of words that we can use to describe our immediate family:

Listen to Track 2.2.8

- ***Madre*** – Mother
- ***Padre*** – Father
- ***Padres*** – Parents
- ***Hermano*** – Brother
- ***Hermana*** – Sister
- ***Hermanos*** – Siblings

Exercise 2.2.2

Listen to Track 2.2.9

In this track, you'll hear a woman talking about her family. Fill in the blanks:

> ***Note:** "*Es*" means "he/she is," "*soy*" means "I am," and "*son*" means "they are." We'll talk more about this in the next lesson. For now, though, just remember these three little words: *Es*, *Soy*, and *Son*.

Mi familia es _____________. Tengo _____________--un hermano y dos hermanas. Mis hermanas son _____________. Mi hermano es _____________. Mi padre es _____________, y mi madre es baja. Mi hermano es _____________, y yo soy _____________ también. Mis hermanas son _____________. Mi hermano es _____________. Yo soy aburrida.

Exercise 2.2.3

Translate the following from English into Spanish:

1. A tall boy - _____________
2. The blue houses- _____________
3. An expensive television- _____________
4. The clean kitchen - _____________
5. Some ugly cats - _____________

Exercise 2.2.4

Now, translate from Spanish into English:

1. *Unos bolígrafos rojos* - _____________
2. *La mujer inteligente* - _____________
3. *Los chicos fuertes* - _____________
4. *Una chica rica* - _____________
5. *El perro gordo* - _____________

Practice Corner

Listening:

Listen to Track 2.2.10

Exercise 2.2.5

Listen to the track and put the sentences in order:

- *padres---mis----simpáticos---muy---son -* _______________________________
- *azules---necesito---bolígrafos---los -* _______________________________
- *y---mi---hermano---fuerte---es---alto -* _______________________________
- *mi---linda---divertida---es---y---madre -* _______________________________

Writing:

Exercise 2.2.6

Write a short description of your immediate family. Use **"mi"** or **"mis"** for "my."

- "Mi" is used with singular things (*Mi hermano* – My brother).
- "Mis" is used with plural things (*Mis hermanos* – My brothers).

And don't forget about **soy** (I am), **es** (he/she is), and **son** (they are).

____

____

Grammar:

Exercise 2.2.7

Correct the following statements so that the adjectives and nouns agree:

Unos gatos feas - _______________________________

Los chico felices - _______________________________

Un país pequeña - _______________________________

Una chica tristes - _______________________________

El hombre delgado - _______________________________

Vocabulary:

Exercise 2.2.8

Translate the phrases from the previous activity from Spanish into English:

1. *Unos gatos feos -* _______________________________
2. *Los chicos felices -* _______________________________
3. *Un país pequeño -* _______________________________
4. *Una chica triste -* _______________________________
5. *El hombre delgado -* _______________________________

A Quick Recap of this Lesson

In this chapter, we discussed adjectives. Here's a recap of what we learned:

- Adjectives in Spanish, like nouns, have both a gender and number.
- The adjective HAS to agree with the noun it's modifying in BOTH gender and number.
- Some adjectives only change from singular to plural, while others will change from singular to plural and masculine to feminine.
- *Usually* the adjective comes AFTER the noun.
- We also learned vocabulary for the immediate family.

ANSWERS:

Exercise 2.2.1

1. La cocina limpia - The clean kitchen
2. Las casas pequeñas - The small houses
3. Las mujeres felices. - The happy women
4. Los edificios feos - The ugly buildings
5. La comida cara -The expensive food
6. Los bolígrafos azules. - The blue pens

Exercise 2.2.2

Mi familia es grande. Tengo tres hermanos--un hermano y dos hermanas. Mis hermanas son lindas. Mi hermano es guapo. Mi padre es alto, y mi madre es baja. Mi hermano es bajo, y yo soy baja también. Mis hermanas son inteligentes. Mi hermano es divertido. Yo soy aburrida.

(My family is big. I have three siblings – one brother and two sisters. My sisters are pretty. My brother is handsome. My dad is tall, and my mom is short. My brother is short, and I am short, too. My sisters are smart. My brother is fun. I am boring.)

Exercise 2.2.3

1. Un chico alto / 2. Las casas azules / 3. Una televisión cara / 4. La cocina limpia / 5. Unos gatos feos

Exercise 2.2.4

1. Some red pens / 2. The smart woman / 3. The strong boys / 4. A rich girl /
5. The fat dog

Exercise 2.2.5

Mis padres son muy simpáticos. (My parents are very nice.)

Necesito los bolígrafos azules. (I need the blue pens.)

Mi hermano es fuerte y alto. (My brother is strong and tall.)

Mi madre es linda y divertida. (My mother is cute and fun.)

Exercise 2.2.6

Example: Mi hermano es alto. Yo soy baja. Mis padres son inteligentes. (My
brother is tall. I am short. My parents are smart.)

Exercise 2.2.7

1. Unos gatos feos (Somo ugly cats)
2. Los chicos felices (The happy boys)
3. Un país pequeño (A small country)
4. Una chica triste (A sad girl)
5. El hombre delgado (The skinny man)

Exercise 2.2.8

1. Some ugly cats / 2. The happy boys / 3. A small country / 4. A sad girl /
5. The skinny man

Week 2, Day 3: *Ser* and *Estar* (An Introduction)

What's in store for you today: *Ser* and Subject Pronouns

Today's goals are:

- To learn about *ser* and *estar* (an introduction)
- To learn the subject pronouns

Listen to Track 2.3.1

Juan: *Hola, me llamo Juan. Soy de Madrid. ¿De dónde eres tú?* (Hello, my name is Juan. I am from Madrid. Where are you from?)

María: *Hola, Juan. Soy María y soy de Buenos Aires.* (Hello, Juan. I am María and I am from Buenos Aires.)

Juan: *¿Por qué estás aquí en España, María?* (Why are you (here) in Spain, María?)

María: *Estoy aquí para visitar a unos amigos.* (I am here to visit some friends.)

Juan: *¿Son tus amigos son españoles?* (Are your friends Spanish?)

María: *Sí. Son de Ávila.* (Yes. They are from Ávila.)

Today, we're going to start looking at how to use two very important verbs in Spanish: ***ser*** and ***estar***. These are probably two of the most frequently used verbs in the Spanish language. They both mean "to be." This means that they can be a little tricky at times. But don't fret! We're going to take our time and work through these together.

Subject Pronouns:

Before we start discussing the whole "***ser*** vs. ***estar***" conundrum, we need to discuss one other little aspect of language: subject pronouns.

These are little words that take the place of the subject. Easy as that. "**María is tall**." "**She is tall**." "**My friends and I are bored**." "**We are bored**."

Here are the subject pronouns in Spanish:

Listen to Track 2.3.2

English Subject Pronoun	Spanish Subject Pronoun
I	*Yo*
You (singular/informal)	*Tú*
He	*Él*
She	*Ella*
You (singular/formal)	*Usted*
We	*Nosotros/ Nosotras*
You (plural/informal)*	*Vosotros*
They	*Ellos/ Ellas*
You (Plural/Formal)	*Ustedes*

*The plural, informal "**you**" form ("***vosotros***") is used only in Spain. In Latin America, the "***ustedes***" is used for all plural "you"s.

I know what you're thinking: "Whoa, what's with all the 'you's?"

Well, if you remember all the way back to Week 1 Day 1, we discussed the difference between <u>formal and informal speech</u> in Spanish. Formal you use with your boss, someone you don't know, etc. (**anyone you want to show respect to**). Informal you use with your family and friends and people you are comfortable with.

In English, we only use one "you" for all of the above situations. Not only for formal and informal, but for plural as well. We do have some fun variations we can use, though (**"y'all"**, **"you guys"**, or even **"youins"**). Think of your plural "**you**"s in Spanish as these.

I'm sure you have another question forming in your mind, and it's probably, "What about the different forms of '**we**' and '**they**'?"

You'll notice that there is a masculine "**we**" (***nosotros***) and a masculine "**they**" (***ellos***) as well as a feminine "**we**" (***nosotras***) and a feminine "**they**" (***ellas***). We use the feminine if we are referring to a group that is made up entirely of females. But if just one male comes along, things change and the masculine form is used.

- **All women** = feminine ending (*-as*)
- **Mixed group** = masculine ending (*-os*)

Exercise 2.3.1

Simple enough: match the Spanish subject pronouns with their English equivalents.

1. *Tú*	1. I
2. *Nosotros/as*	2. You (singular/informal)
3. *Él*	3. He
4. *Usted*	4. She
5. *Yo*	5. You (singular/formal)
6. *Ella*	6. We
7. *Ellos/as*	7. You (plural/informal)
8. *Ustedes*	8. They
9. *Vosotros*	9. You (plural/formal)

Ser vs. Estar

Remember: today's lesson is an <u>introduction</u> to these verbs. This means that you don't have to worry about memorizing all the rules right away. Just make sure that you understand the concepts and basic differences between them! Over the next few days, we'll go into more detail, don't worry.

Ser

Listen to Track 2.3.3

The first way to say "to be" that we'll look at is **ser**, and it's used for <u>permanent</u> qualities.

- *Soy de Madrid.* (I am from Madrid.)
- *Ella es Ana.* (She is Ana.)
- *Somos amigos.* (We are friends.)

We conjugate* **ser** like this:

*Conjugating basically means "**changing the verb to make it match the subject**." In English, we do this, just not as much as in Spanish. For example, "I run" vs. "he run<u>s</u>," or even "I am" vs. "you are" vs. "he is."

In Spanish, each "person" (1st person, 2nd person, etc.) will have its own conjugation.

Listen to Track 2.3.4

Yo soy (I am)	***Nosotros/as somos*** (We are)
Tú eres (You are)	***Vosotros/as sois*** (You are)
Él/Ella/Usted es (He / she / you)	***Ellos/as/Ustedes son*** (They are you)

Notice how the verbs have been put into a handy little chart. From today onwards, when we learn a new verb, you'll find it conjugated to match its subject, and put into this chart. Here's how it works:

Yo (i.e. 1st person singular)	***Nosotros/as*** (i.e. 1st person plural)
Tú (i.e. 2nd person singular)	***Vosotros*** (i.e. 2nd person)
Él/Ella/Usted (i.e. 3rd person singular)	***Ellos/as/Ustedes*** (i.e. 3rd person plural)

The only exceptions to these placements are the "***Usted***" and "***Ustedes***" forms, which, although they are technically the 2nd person, will follow the same conjugations as the 3rd persons.

If you were hoping for an easy way to remember when to use *ser*, we have one for you! Think of the acronym "DOCTOR."

- **D**ate
- **O**ccupation (a job title, like "doctor," for example)
- **C**haracteristic (Is he tall? Are they nice people? Is she funny?)
- **T**ime
- **O**rigin (Where are you from?)
- **R**elation (How do you know this person? Friend? Family?)

You'll notice that most of these (with the exception of the date and time) are things that usually don't change about someone or something. They're all situations in which you need to describe something that is generally pretty consistent. (My mother will always be my mother. I am a teacher. My sister is short. I am, and always will be, from the United States.)

Exercise 2.3.2

Conjugate **_ser_**:

Yo	Nosotros/as
Tú	*Vosotros/as*
Él/Ella/Usted	*Ellos/as/Ustedes*

Estar 2

Listen to Track 2.3.5

The second way to say "to be" is with the verb **_estar_**. This is used for <u>temporary</u> things.

- **_Estoy en la tienda_**. (I am in the store.)
- **_Él está triste_**. (He is sad.)
- **_Ellos están felices_**. (They are happy.)

The conjugations for **_Estar_** look like this:

Yo estoy (I am)	*Nosotros/as estamos* (We are)
Tú estás (You're)	*Vosotros/as estáis* (You are)
Él/Ella/Usted está (He / she / you are)	*Ellos/as/Ustedes están* (They are)

Again, we have a fun little acronym you can use for remembering when you should use **_estar_**. Just remember the word "PLACE."

- **Position** (The dog is next to the couch.)
- **Location** (I am in the store.)
- **Action** (Present progressive – we'll get to this later.)
- **Condition** (I am tired.)
- **Emotion** (I am happy.)

Again, take a moment to notice the type of things that are being talked about with *estar*. They are things that will most likely change frequently. (I'm not always going to be sitting at the table. My friend won't be at work forever. I'm tired now but after I take a nap, I won't be. And just because I'm happy at the moment doesn't mean I'll be happy in an hour.)

Exercise 2.3.3

Conjugate *estar*:

Estar

Yo	*Nosotros/as*
Tú	*Vosotros/as*
Él/Ella/Usted	*Ellos/as/Ustedes*

Exercise 2.3.4

Look at the following adjectives (some of them will be new for you) and decide if you would use *ser* or *estar* with them.

1. *Alto* – Tall : _____________
2. *Delgado* – Skinny : _____________
3. *Enfadado* – Angry : _____________
4. *Limpio* – Clean : _____________
5. *Lindo* – Pretty : _____________
6. *Tímido* – Shy : _____________
7. *Sucio* – Dirty : _____________
8. *Emocionado* – Excited : _______
9. *Cansado* – Tired : _____________
10. *Divertido* – Fun : _____________

Something to Note:

Sometimes, both *ser* and *estar* are viable options to use with an adjective. In order to decide which one to use, you need to ask yourself one important question:

- Am I describing an <u>intrinsic</u> quality of something?

If you are, then use **ser**. If not, use **estar**.

Listen to Track 2.3.6

For example:

- **La sopa está fría** (The soup is cold, i.e. it's supposed to be a hot soup, but now it is cold. "Cold" is not an intrinsic quality of the soup.)
- **Mi madre es feliz** (My mother is a happy person. I can use the word "happy" to describe her.)
- **Mi hermano es perezoso** (My brother is lazy – he's a lazy person.)
- **Hoy, estoy perezosa** (Today, I'm feeling lazy – it's a condition I'm feeling today, but it isn't a permanent quality of who I am.)

Some adjectives will change meaning depending on if they're being used with *ser* or *estar*. Here are four very common examples:

Listen to Track 2.3.7

Adjective	Meaning with **Ser**	Meaning with **Estar**
Aburrido	Boring	Bored
Rico	Rich	Tasty (for food)
Listo*	Intelligent/Clever	Ready
Malo	Evil	Sick

*This is a new vocabulary word for you, and one worth taking note of.

Exercise 2.3.5

Translate the following sentences from Spanish into English. As you write the sentences down, make sure to make a note of why either *ser* or *estar* is being used. What is the meaning/reason behind it?

1. *Mi hermano es muy listo.*

   - _______________________________

2. *Mis padres están enfadados .*

   - _______________________________

3. *Mis amigos son divertidos.*

   - _______________________________

4. *Nosotros estamos tristes.*

   - _______________________________

5. *Tú estás nervioso .*

   - _______________________________

6. *Yo soy nervioso.*

   - _______________________________

7. *Yo estoy enferma.*

   - _______________________________

8. *Ella es mala.*

   - _______________________________

9. *El profesor es aburrido. Yo estoy aburrido.*

   - _______________________________

Practice Corner

Listening:

Listen to Track 2.3.8

Exercise 2.3.6

María está en una fiesta. Ella ha conocido a una mujer llamada Lucía, y están hablando de sus familias y amigos. (María is at a party. She has met a woman named Lucía and they are talking about their families and friends.)

Listen to the track and answer the questions (try to answer in complete sentences):

- *¿De dónde es María?* (Where is María from?)

  ____

- *¿De dónde es Lucía?* (Where is Lucía from?)

  ____

- *¿Cómo es el hermano de María?* (What is María's brother like?)

  ____

- *¿Cómo es la madre de María?* (What is María's mother like?)

  ____

- *¿Dónde está el hermano de Lucía?* (Where is Lucía's brother?)

  ____

- *¿Está feliz allí?* (Is he happy there?)

  ____

Writing:

Exercise 2.3.7

Write out a short description for each of the following prompts (pay attention to whether you're using *ser* or *estar* and conjugate the verb according to the subject:

- *Mis amigos y yo somos* (My friends and I are)_____________________________.
- *Ahora mismo estoy en* (Right now I am at)_____________________________.
- *Yo soy* (I am)_____________________________.

- *Mi mejor amigo(a) es* (My best friend is) _______________________________.
- *Mis amigos están* (My friends are)_______________________________.

Grammar/Vocabulary:

Exercise 2.3.8

For each of the following adjectives, decide if you should use *ser* or *estar*, or if both can be used (depending on the situation), and why:

- *Grande* – Large : _______________
- *Pequeño* – Small: _______________
- *Gordo* – Fat: _______________
- *Delgado* – Slim: _______________
- *Malo* – Bad: _______________
- *Aburrido* – Bored: _______________
- *Débil* – Weak : _______________

A Quick Recap of this Lesson

Today, we talked about *ser* and *estar*. We discussed that:

- We use *ser* for <u>permanent qualities</u>.
- We use *estar* for <u>temporary states</u>.

We also talked about how adjectives are used with *ser* and *estar*:

- If we are describing something <u>intrinsic</u>, we will use *ser*.
  - ***Mi madre es feliz.*** (My mother is happy.)
    - I.e. She is a happy person.

- If we are describing a condition, we use *estar*.
  - ***Mi madre está feliz.*** (My mother is happy.)
    - I.e. We are talking about her emotions. She is happy right now.

- We also looked at four adjectives specifically that change meaning with *ser* and *estar*:

Adjective	Meaning with **Ser**	Meaning with **Estar**
Aburrido	Boring	Bored
Rico	Rich	Tasty (for food)
Listo *	Intelligent/Clever	Ready
Malo	Evil	Sick

ANSWERS:

Exercise 2.3.1

1. Tú - 2. You (singular/familiar)
2. Nosotros/as - 6. We
3. Él - 3. He
4. Usted - 5. You (singular/formal)
5. Yo - 1. I
6. Ella - 4. She
7. Ellos/as - 8. They
8. Ustedes - 7. You (plural/familiar)
9. Vosotros - 9. You (plural/formal)

Exercise 2.3.2

Yo soy (I am)	Nosotros/as somos (We are)
Tú eres (You are)	Vosotros/as sois (You are)
Él/ Ella/ Usted es (He / she / you)	Ellos/as/Ustedes son (They are you)

Exercise 2.3.3

Yo estoy (I am)	Nosotros/as estamos (We are)
Tú estás (You are)	Vosotros /as estáis (You are)
Él/Ella/Usted está (He / she / you are)	Ellos/as/Ustedes están (They are)

Exercise 2.3.4

1. Ser, 2. Ser, 3. Estar, 4. Estar, 5. Ser, 6. Ser, 7. Estar, 8. Estar, 9. Estar, 10. Ser

Exercise 2.3.5

1. My brother is very clever/intelligent.
2. My parents are angry (estar because they are not "angry people").
3. My friends are fun (ser because they are "fun people").
4. We are sad (estar because it's an emotion; we're not always sad).
5. You are nervous (estar because you are not a "nervous person").
6. I am nervous (ser because I'm a "nervous person").

7. I am sick.
8. She is evil.
9. The teacher is boring. I am bored.

Exercise 2.3.6

- María es de Madrid. (María is from Madrid.)
- Lucía es de México. (Lucia is from Mexico.)
- Él es muy inteligente. (He is very smart.)
- Ella es linda y divertida. (She is cute and fun.)
- Él está en Nueva York. (He is in New York.)
- Si está feliz allí. (He/She is happy there.)

Transcript:

María: Hola, Lucía. Yo soy María. Mi familia y yo somos de Madrid. ¿De dónde eres? (Hello, Lucía. I am María. My family and I are from Madrid. Where are you from?)

Lucía: Yo soy de México. (I am from Mexico.)

María: Mi hermano está en México. Trabaja allí. Él es muy inteligente. (My brother is in Mexico. He works there. He is very smart.)

Lucía: Y, ¿Cómo son tus padres? (And what are your parents like?)

María: Mi padre es alto y fuerte. Mi madre es linda y divertida. ¿Cómo es tu familia? (My father is tall and strong. My mother is pretty and fun. What is your family like?)

Lucía: Mis hermanos son muy divertidos. Mi hermana es lista pero aburrida. Mi hermano está en Nueva York ahora. Él está feliz allí. (My brothers are very fun. My sister is smart but boring. My brother is in New York now. He is happy there.)

Exercise 2.3.7

Sample answers:

- Mis amigos y yo somos felices. (My friends and I are happy.)
- Ahora mismo estoy en la cocina. (Right now I am in the kitchen.)
- Yo soy baja, lista y divertida. (I am short, smart and fun.)
- Mi mejor amiga es inteligente. (My best friend is smart.)
- Mis amigos están en casa. (My friends are at home.)

Exercise 2.3.8

- Grande – *ser* ("big" is an intrinsic quality of something.)
- Pequeños – **ser** ("small" is an intrinsic quality of something.)
- Gordo – **ser** ("fat" is an intrinsic quality of something.)
- Delgado – **ser** ("skinny" is an intrinsic quality of something.)
- Malo – **BOTH** (with **ser**, "malo" means "evil," and with **estar** it means "sick.")
- Aburrido – **BOTH** (with **ser**, "aburrido" means "boring," and with **estar** it means "bored.")
- Débil – **ser** ("weak" is an intrinsic quality of something.)

Week 2, Day 4: More about *Ser*

What's in store for you today: Working with the verb ser

Listen to Track 2.4.1

In the track below, listen to a woman briefly describe herself and a friend.

Hola. Yo soy Lucía. Soy muy tímida. Mi amigo César no es tímido. Es muy extrovertido. Yo soy de Barcelona. César es mexicano. Yo soy abogada. César es médico. Somos muy amigos.

(Hello, I am Lucía. I am very shy. My friend César is not shy. He is very outgoing. I am from Barcelona. César is Mexican. I am a lawyer. César is a doctor. We are very good friends.)

In today's lesson, we're going to focus on the verb *ser*. As you remember, we already discussed how *ser* is used with intrinsic qualities (i.e. permanent characteristics). Today, we're going to expand on that.

Before we get too far ahead, let's review the conjugation of the verb *ser*.

Listen to Track 2.4.2

Yo soy (I am)	*Nosotros/as somos* (We are)
Tú eres (You are)	*Vosotros/as sois* (You are)
Él/Ella/Usted es (He / she / you)	*Ellos/as/Ustedes son* (They are you)

Doctor! Doctor! Give me a clue...

Yesterday, we looked at a fun little acronym for when we should use the verb **ser**. Here it is:

- **D**ate
- **O**ccupation (a job title, like "doctor," for example)
- **C**haracteristic (Is he tall? Are they nice people? Is she funny?)
- **T**ime
- **O**rigin (Where are you from?)
- **R**elation (How do you know this person? Friend? Family? Co-worker?)

Listen to Track 2.4.3

For today's lesson, we're going to expand on two of these points specifically: **occupation** and **characteristics**. We've already discussed **origin** (I am from...). And wc have seen **relation** used throughout a lot of our lessons ("*Él es mi hermano*" [*He is my brother.*] although we will talk more about this in a few days). **Date** and **time** we will look at later on.

Yo soy médico...

Listen to Track 2.4.4

First, let's talk about **occupations**. Here is a list of some of the most common occupations in Spanish. (Be warned! This is a long list. But you'll notice that an awful lot of these words look and sound pretty similar to words in English. So some of them shouldn't be too difficult.)

- ***Abogado/a*** – Lawyer
- ***Arquitecto/a*** – Architect
- ***Bombero/a*** – Firefighter
- ***Camarero/a*** – Waiter/Waitress
- ***Científico/a*** – Scientist
- ***Cocinero/a*** – Chef
- ***Contable*** – Accountant
- ***Electricista*** – Electrician
- ***Enfermero/a*** – Nurse
- ***Estudiante*** – Student
- ***Fontanero/a*** – Plumber
- ***Granjero/a*** – Farmer
- ***Médico/a*** – Doctor
- ***Oficinista*** – Office worker
- ***Periodista*** – Journalist
- ***Piloto**** – Pilot
- ***Policía*** – Police officer
- ***Profesor/Profesora*** – Teacher

- ***Recepcionista*** – Receptionist
- ***Secretario/a*** – Secretary
- ***Soldado**** – Soldier
- ***Taxista*** – Taxi driver
- ***Vendedor/Vendedora*** – Salesperson
- ***Veterinario/a*** – Vet

Note: Don't see your profession listed here? Let us know so we can add it to our list!

Am I a *"dentista"* or a *"dentisto"*?

Listen to Track 2.4.5

Let's take a moment to talk about a few grammar points that we're going to want to remember when talking about professions.

- First, some of our professions will change **gender** based on if the speaker is a man or a woman.
  - ***Yo soy veterinario. Yo soy veterinaria.*** (I am a vet. I am veterinary.)
  - ***Yo soy profesor. Yo soy profesora.*** (I am a teacher. I am a teacher.)

- Professions that end in *-o*, or a consonant, will change.
  - *-o* becomes an *-a*
    - ***Bombero*** - Firefighter
    - ***Bombera*** - Firefighter
  - If it ends in a consonant, add an *-a* to the end.
    - ***Vendedor*** - Seller
    - ***Vendedora*** - Saleswoman

*There are exceptions to this rule:
  - **Piloto** will not change (only the article).
    - ***El piloto*** - The pilot
    - ***La piloto*** - The pilot
  - **Soldado** will not change (only the article).
    - ***El soldado*** - The soldier
    - ***La soldado*** - The soldier

- Professions that end in *-ista*, *-ia*, and *-e*, will **not** change (gender).
  - ○ ***Mi hermano es dentista.*** - My brother is a dentist.
  - ○ ***Mi hermana es dentista.*** - My sister is a dentist.
  - ○ ***Nosotros somos policías.*** - We are police.
  - ○ ***Ellos son taxistas.*** - They are taxi drivers.
  - ○ ***Tú eres estudiante.*** - You are a student.

- Lastly, <u>unlike in English, we will **not** use an indefinite article when talking about our profession.</u>
  - ○ ***Yo soy profesora.*** (NOT Yo soy una profesora.) - I am a teacher.
  - ○ ***Nosotras somos granjeras.*** - We are farmers.
  - ○ ***Él es bombero.*** - He is a firefighter.

Exercise 2.4.1

Listen to Track 2.4.6

Listen and fill in the blanks:

Yo trabajo en _______________. *Yo soy* _______________. *Mi hermano es* _______________, *y mi padre es* _______________. *Mi madre trabaja en un hospital. Ella es* _______________. *Mi hermana es* _______________.

¿Cómo soy? What am I like?

One of the times you'll find yourself using *ser* the most is to **describe** yourself, other people, and the places around you. We already have a good list of adjectives going that we can use to accomplish this. But today, let's grow that list just a little, shall we?

Listen to Track 2.4.7

- ***Interesante*** – Interesting
- ***Trabajador/a*** – Hardworking
- ***Valiente*** – Brave
- ***Cobarde*** – Cowardly
- ***Generoso/a*** – Generous
- ***Honesto/a*** – Honest
- ***Callado/a*** – Quiet
- ***Hablador/a*** – Talkative
- ***Contento*** – Content/Happy
- ***Infeliz*** – Discontented
- ***Joven*** – Young
- ***Mayor*** – Old
- ***Tímido/a*** – Shy
- ***Extrovertido/a*** – Outgoing

Exercise 2.4.2

Translate the following sentences from Spanish into English:

1. *Yo no soy una persona infeliz.*

   - ____

2. *Mi padre es extrovertido, pero mi madre es tímida.*

   - ____

3. *Mis hermanos son jóvenes*.*

   - ____

4. *Mi mejor (best) amigo no es muy (very) trabajador.*

   - ____

5. *Alejandra es honesta y generosa.*

   - ____

6. *Ricardo es bastante (rather) hablador.*

   - ____

*In case you were wondering, there is an accent on this word to keep the original pronunciation correct. In *"joven"* the stress falls on the syllable *"jo"* (because it ends in a consonant, and the stress falls on the second to last syllable, as we learned before). When we add the *-es*, we see that suddenly, the second to last syllable is different. Now, it's *"ve."* But we want to keep the original pronunciation, so we need to add an accent to clarify that (since it's no longer following the rule).

When we add the *-es*, we see that suddenly, the second to last syllable is different. Now, it's *"ve."* But we want to keep the original pronunciation, so we need to add an accent to clarify that (since it's no longer following the rule).

Rules to remember:

Listen to Track 2.4.8

Like with the adjectives we saw before, we need to make sure that our adjectives agree with the subject in **number** and **gender.**

- ***Nosotros somos tímidos.*** (We are shy.)
- ***Ellos son valientes.*** (They are brave.)
- ***Nosotras somos trabajadoras.*** (We are hardworking.)

Practice Corner

Listening:

Exercise 2.4.3

Listen to Track 2.4.9

Listen and put the sentences in order:

1. *no---es---Pedro---trabajador* - ___________________________
2. *mis---son---inteligentes---muy---amigos* - ___________________________
3. *no---soy---yo---extrovertido---muy* - ___________________________
4. *contentas---personas----nosotros---somos* - ___________________________
5. *el---no---profesor---es---mayor* - ___________________________

Writing/Vocabulary:

For each adjective we learned today, try to create a sentence describing someone you know:

Example: *Mi profesor es interesante. Mis padres son trabajadores. Mi hermano es joven. Yo soy valiente. Mis amigos son honestos.* (My teacher is interesting. My parents are hardworking. My brother is young. I am brave. My friends are honest.)

- *Interesante*
- *Trabajador/a*
- *Valiente*
- *Cobarde*
- *Generoso/a*

- *Honesto/a*
- *Callado/a*
- *Hablador/a*
- *Contento*
- *Infeliz*

- *Joven*
- *Mayor*
- *Tímido/a*
- *Extrovertido/a*

Grammar:

Exercise 2.4.4

Fill in the blanks with the correct forms of the verb *ser*.

- *Yo _________ de Colombia.* (I _________ from Colombia.)
- *Mis amigos _________ muy divertidos.* (My friends _________ very funny.)
- *Ella _________ callada.* (She _________ quiet.)
- *Miguel y sus amigos no _____ cobardes.* (Miguel and his friends are not coward.)
- *Tú _________ valiente.* (You _________ brave.)
- *Mi familia y yo _________ trabajadores.* (My family and I _________ workers.)

A Quick Recap of this Lesson

Today, we talked about using *ser* to describe permanent qualities:

- **Professions**:
    - We talked about making the profession agree with the person being talked about:
        - ***Bombero – bombera*** (Firefighter – masculine and feminine)
        - ***Fontanero – Fontanera*** (Plumber – masculine and feminine)
    - We also talked about how we <u>will not use</u> an indirect article with professions:
        - ***Yo soy oficinista.*** (I am an office worker.)
        - ***Tú eres camarero.*** (You are a waiter.)
- **Personality**:
    - We learned some new adjectives to describe people.

ANSWERS:

Exercise 2.4.1

Yo trabajo en una cocina. Yo soy cocinero. Mi hermano es policía, y mi padre es contable. Mi madre trabaja en un hospital. Ella es enfermera. Mi hermana es estudiante.

(I work in a kitchen. I am a chef. My brother is a police officer, and my dad is an accountant. My mother works in a hospital. She is a nurse. My sister is a student.)

Exercise 2.4.2

1. I am not an unhappy person.
2. My father is outgoing, but my mother is shy.
3. My brothers are young.
4. My best friend isn't very hardworking.
5. Alejandra is honest and generous.
6. Ricardo is rather talkative (a rather talkative person).

Exercise 2.4.3

1. Pedro no es trabajador. (Pedro is not a worker.)
2. Mis amigos son muy inteligentes. (My friends are very smart.)
3. Yo no soy muy extrovertido. (I am not very outgoing.)
4. Nosotros somos personas contentas. (We are happy people)
5. El profesor no es mayor. The teacher is not older)

Exercise 2.4.4

- Yo soy de Colombia. (I am from Colombia.)
- Mis amigos son muy divertidos. (My friends are very funny.)
- Ella es callada. (She is quiet.)
- Miguel y sus amigos no son cobardes. (Miguel and his friends are not coward.)
- Tú eres valiente. (You are brave.)
- Mi familia y yo somos trabajadores. (My family and I arc workers.)

Week 2, Day 5: More with *Ser* and Introduction to *Tener*

What's in store for you today: More work with **ser** and learning the verb **tener**

> ### Today's goals are:
>
> - To learn more about *ser*
> - To learn about the verb *tener*
> - To learn vocabulary to describe people (physically)

Listen to Track 2.5.1

María: *Yo me parezco mucho a mi padre.*

Ángela: *Ah, ¿sí? ¿Y cómo es tu padre?*

María: *Mi padre tiene el pelo castaño, es alto y tiene los ojos marrones. ¿Cómo es tu padre?*

Angela: *Mi padre es de estatura mediana, rubio, y tiene los ojos verdes. Yo me parezco a mi madre. Ella es baja, pelirroja, y tiene los ojos azules.*

Before we move on to working with *estar*, let's work a little bit more with the verb *ser* and expand our descriptive abilities a little bit more. Today, we're going to discuss how to talk about <u>physical</u> qualities.

Ser... Tener...

Listen to Track 2.5.2

When describing people's physical appearance in Spanish, like in English, we use two different verbs: **ser** (to be) and **tener** (to have).

Listen to Track 2.5.3

Some of the adjectives we'll use with **ser** you already know:

"*Yo soy alto. Nosotros somos bajos.*"

Below, you'll find a list of some other qualities we'll mention using the verb **ser**:

- **Pelirrojo/a** - Redhead
- **Rubio/a** - Blond
- **Calvo/a** - Bald
- **De estatura mediana** - Of medium height

Exercise 2.5.1

Read the sentences below and choose if each one is **verdadero** (true) or **falso** (false) <u>as they relate to you</u>. For the ones that are false, write out **una oración verdadera** (a true sentence).

Examples:

V/F **Yo soy de estatura mediana.**(I am of medium height.)

Mi respuesta (my answer): **Falso – Yo soy baja.** (False - I am short.)

V/F **Yo soy pelirrojo/a.** (I am a redhead.)

Mi respuesta: **Verdad – Yo soy pelirroja.** (True - I am a redhead.)

1. V/F **Yo soy alto/a.** (I am tall.)
   a. *Mi respuesta* (My answer): _______________________
2. V/F **Mi padre es calvo.** (My father is bald.)
   a. *Mi respuesta* (My answer): _______________________
3. V/F **Mi mejor amigo** (my best friend) **es de estatura mediana** (is of medium height).
   a. *Mi respuesta* (My answer): _______________________

Tener...

There are still a lot of descriptions missing from our running list! What if you have brown hair? How do you say, "**I have hazel eyes**"? Let's look at that right now!

Listen to Track 2.5.4

In order to talk about other physical qualities, we're going to need to use the verb **tener**. This means "to have." We need it to say **tengo el pelo largo** (I have long hair) or **tengo una barba** (I have a beard).

Here's how it conjugates:

Yo tengo (I have)	**Nosotros/as tenemos** (we have)
Tú tienes (you – familiar, singular – have)	**Vosotros/as tenéis** (you – plural, familiar) have
Él/Ella/Usted tiene (he/she/you – singular, formal – have)	**Ellos/as/Ustedes tienen** (they/you – plural, formal – have)

Exercise 2.5.2

Let's practice this new verb and review some old vocabulary at the same time! Translate the following sentences from Spanish into English:

1. *Yo tengo tres manzanas.* - _______________________________
2. *Nosotros tenemos cinco televisiones.* - _______________________________
3. *Ellos tienen una casa grande.* - _______________________________
4. *Ella tiene un perro pequeño.* - _______________________________
5. *Tú tienes un amigo simpático.* - _______________________________

¿Qué tengo? (What do I have?)

Listen to Track 2.5.5

Here is a list of vocabulary you can use with *tener* to describe people's physical appearance:

- **Pelo** – Hair
  - **Largo** – Long
  - **Corto** – Short
  - **Medio largo** – Medium length
  - **Oscuro** – Dark
  - **Castaño*** – Brown
  - **Rizado** – Curly
  - **Liso** – Straight
  - **Canoso** – Gray
- **Ojos** – eyes
  - **Azules** – Blue
  - **Verdes** – Green
  - **De color avellana** – Hazel
  - **Marrones*** – Brown
- **La barba** – The beard
- **El bigote** – The mustache

* I can hear your question: "Why two 'brown's?" Well, the answer is, there's not a real answer. It just depends on the variety of Spanish being spoken. In some places, "*marrón*" is used for both, while in others, they are used separately (**as they're shown here**). It's a good idea to be familiar with both options.

Exercise 2.5.3

Translate the following sentences from Spanish into English (and look out for more vocabulary review!):

1. *El camarero tiene pelo corto.* - _______________________________________
2. *Tú tienes ojos de color avellana* - _______________________________________
3. *Lucía y su madre tienen pelo largo y oscuro.* - _______________________________
4. *Mi novio tiene una barba.* - _______________________________________
5. *Yo tengo un bigote.* - _______________________________________
6. *Nosotros tenemos el pelo rizado.* - _______________________________________
7. *El médico tiene pelo canoso.* - _______________________________________
8. *La contable tiene pelo liso y castaño.* - _______________________________

Exercise 2.5.4

Describe the picture:

Image via Pixabay

Ella tiene

Ella es

Practice Corner

Listening:

Listen to Track 2.5.6

Exercise 2.5.5

Listen and answer the questions:

María está hablando de su familia y amigos. (María is talking about her family and friends.)

1. *El padre de María NO es...* (Maria's father is NOT ...)
    a. Alto   b. Delgado   c. Débil   d. Calvo
2. *La madre de María tiene...* (Maria's mother has ...)
    a. Pelo canoso   b. Ojos verdes   c. Pelo liso   d. Ojos marrones
3. *El hermano de María...* (Mary's brother ...)
    a. Tiene barba   b. Es alto   c. Tiene bigote   d. Es pelirrojo
4. *María...*
    a. Es rubia b. Tiene pelo rizado   c. Es alta   d. Tiene ojos verdes

Writing:

Exercise 2.5.6

Write out a description of yourself and two other people you know.

Sample answer:

Yo soy baja. Tengo pelo largo. Soy rubia. Mi mejor amiga tiene pelo corto. Ella tiene pelo castaño. Yo tengo ojos azules. Mi mejor amigo tiene ojos marrones. (I am short. I have long hair. I am blond. My best [female] friend has short hair. She has brown hair. I have blue eyes. My best [male] friend has brown eyes.)

____

____

Grammar:

Conjugate ***ser***:

Yo _____ (I am)	***Nosotros*** _________ (We are)
Tú _______ (You are)	***Vosotros/as*** _______ (You are)
El/Ella/Usted ______ (He/She is / You are)	***Ellos/Ustedes*** ______ (They/You are)

Conjugate **tener**:

Yo _________ (I have)	***Nosotros*** ___________ (We have)
Tú _________ (You have)	***Vosotros*** _________ (You have)
El/Ella/Usted _________ (He/She has / You have)	***Ellos/Ustedes*** _________ (They/You have)

Vocabulary:

Exercise 2.5.7

What do the following mean in English?

1. *Rubio* - ________________
2. *Bigote* - ________________
3. *Pelo medio largo* - ________________
4. *Ojos marrones* - ________________
5. *Calvo* - ________________
6. *Pelo rizado* - ________________
7. *Pelo castaño* - ________________
8. *Pelo canoso* - ________________
9. *Pelirrojo* - ________________
10. *Ojos de color avellana* -___________

A Quick Recap of this Lesson

Today, we talked about how to describe people physically.

- We learned some new vocabulary (***pelirrojo*** – redhead, ***calvo*** – bald, etc.).
- We learned about the verb ***tener*** (to have):
  - We learned vocabulary to use with this verb:
    - ***Pelo*** (Hair)
    - ***Ojos*** (Eyes)
    - ***Barba*** (Beard)
    - ***Bigote*** (Mustache)

ANSWERS:

Exercise 2.5.1

1. Falso – Yo soy baja. (False – I am short.)
2. Verdadero – Mi padre es calvo. (True – My father is bald)
3. Falso – Mi mejor amigo es alto. (False – My best friend is tall.

Exercise 2.5.2

1. I have three apples.
2. We have five televisions.
3. They have a big house.
4. She has a small dog.
5. You have a nice friend.

Exercise 2.5.3

1. The waiter has short hair.
2. You have hazel eyes.
3. Lucía and her mother have long, dark hair.
4. My boyfriend has a beard.
5. I have a mustache.
6. We have curly hair.
7. The doctor has gray hair.
8. The accountant has straight, brown hair.

Exercise 2.5.4

Ella tiene pelo corto y oscuro, tiene ojos color avellana. (She has short and dark hair, she has hazel eyes.)

Ella es de mediana estatura. (She is medium height)

Exercise 2.5.5

1. C (Calvo) C (Débil) OR D (Calvo)
2. D (Ojos marrones)
3. C (Tiene bigote
4. B (Tiene pelo rizado.)

Transcript:

Mi familia es interesante. Mi padre es muy alto. Él es delgado y calvo. Mi madre es de estatura mediana. Ella tiene pelo castaño y ojos marrones. También, ella es gorda. Mi hermano tiene bigote pero no tiene barba. Él es bajo y rubio y tiene pelo liso. Yo soy pelirroja y tengo ojos azules. Yo tengo pelo rizado.

(My family is interesting. My dad is very tall. He is skinny and bald. My mother is medium height. She has brown hair and brown eyes. Also, she is fat. My brother has a mustache but doesn't have a beard. He is short and blond and has straight hair. I am a redhead and have blue eyes. I have curly hair.)

Exercise 2.5.6

Conjugate **ser**:

Yo soy (I am)	Nosotros somos (We are)
Tú eres (You are)	Vosotros sois (You are)
El/Ella/Usted es (He/She is / You are)	Ellos/Ustedes son (They/You are)

Conjugate **tener**:

Yo tengo (I have)	Nosotros tenemos (We have)
Tú tienes (You have)	Vosotros tenéis (You have)
El/Ella/Usted tiene (He/She has / You have)	Ellos/Ustedes tienen (They/You have)

Exercise 2.5.7

1. Blond
2. Mustache
3. Medium-length hair
4. Brown eyes
5. Bald
6. Curly hair
7. Brown hair
8. Gray hair
9. Redhead
10. Hazel eyes

Week 2 Recap

This week, we learned about articles, adjectives, and we talked about *ser* and *estar*. Let's take some time to go over everything before we move on to Week 3.

Listening:

Listen to Track WR 2.1

Exercise WR 2.1

Listen to the track and answer the questions:

1. *¿Qué NO necesita comprar en la tienda?* (What he does NOT need to buy in the store?)
   a. La carne de vaca (the beef)   c. La carne de cerdo (the pork)
   b. Las zanahorias (the carrots)   d. Las patatas (the potatoes)

2. *¿Cuántas cebollas necesita?* (How many onions does he need?)
   a. Dos (two)   b. Tres (three)   c. Cuatro (four)   d. Una (one)

3. *¿Qué necesita para el postre?* (What does he need for the dessert?)
   a. Manzanas (apples)   c. Plátanos (bananas)
   b. Uvas (grapes)   d. Naranjas (oranges)

Listen to Track WR 2.2

Exercise WR 2.2

Listen to the track and answer the questions (using complete sentences):

1. *¿Tiene la hermana de Juana pelo largo?* (Does Juana's sister have long hair?)
   -____

2. *¿Es la hermana de Juana pelirroja?* (Is Juana's sister a redhead?)
   -____

3. *¿Cómo es el padre de Ricardo?* (What is Ricardo's father like?)
   -____

4. *¿Qué hace el padre de Ricardo?* (What does Ricardo's father do?)
   -____

5. *¿Qué hace la hermana de Juana?* (What does Juana's sister do?)

    -____

Ricardo y Juana están en una fiesta. Están hablando de algunos miembros de sus familias que están allí también. (Ricardo and Juana are at a party. They are talking about some members of their families that are there as well.)

Writing:

Exercise WR 2.3

Write a description of yourself and another person in your family. Describe personality and physical characteristics.

____

____

____

Exercise WR 2.4

Answer the following questions in complete sentences.

1. *¿Dónde estás ahora mismo?* (Where are you right now?)

    -____

2. *¿Tienes hermanos?* (Do you have siblings?)

    -____

3. *¿Estás triste o feliz ahora mismo?* (Are you happy or sad right now?)

    -____

4. *¿Eres muy hablador?* (Are you very talkative?)

    -____

5. *¿Eres extrovertido?* (Are you outgoing?)

    -____

Grammar:

Exercise WR 2.5

How do you say the following in Spanish?

1. The short girls - ______________________

2. The big country - _____________________
3. An ugly dog - _____________________
4. A fat cat - _____________________
5. Some weak men - _____________________
6. The boring teacher - _____________________
7. The yellow house - _____________________

Exercise WR 2.6

Explain the difference between the sentences in each set (i.e. what do they mean?):

Set 1: a. *Yo soy infeliz.*   b. *Yo estoy infeliz.*

____

Set 2: a. *Ella está lista.*   b. *Ella es lista.*

____

Set 3: a. *Nosotros estamos aburridos.*   b. *Nosotros somos aburridos.*

____

Set 4: a. *Ellos son malos.*   b. *Ellos están malos.*

____

Exercise WR 2.7

Fill in the blanks with the correct forms of *ser* or *tener*.

1. *Yo _____________ pelo medio-largo.*
2. *Nosotros _____________ de Inglaterra.*
3. *Ellos _____________ ojos marrones.*
4. *Mi padre _____________ bigote.*
5. *Tú _____________ muy alto.*
6. *Mis amigos _____________ honestos.*
7. *Ellas _____________ valientes.*
8. *Nosotros _____________ pelo rizado*

Vocabulary:

Exercise WR 2.8

Translate the sentences from the last activity from Spanish into English:

1. *Yo tengo pelo medio-largo.* - _______________________________________
2. *Nosotros somos de Inglaterra.* - _______________________________________
3. *Ellos tienen ojos marrones.* - _______________________________________
4. *Mi padre tiene bigote.* - _______________________________________
5. *Tú eres muy alto.* - _______________________________________
6. *Mis amigos son honestos.* - _______________________________________
7. *Ellas son valientes.* - _______________________________________
8. *Nosotros tenemos pelo rizado.-* _______________________________________

ANSWERS:

Exercise WR 2.1:

1. C (la carne de cerdo) / 2. B (tres) / 3. D (naranjas)

Transcript:

Hombre: Hoy, ceno con mis amigos en mi casa. Necesito comprar unas cosas para preparar la cena. Necesito comprar tres cebollas y dos zanahorias. También, necesito comprar la carne de vaca y cuatro patatas. Para terminar, necesito unas naranjas para el postre.

(Today, I am having dinner with my friends in my house. I need to buy some things in order to prepare the dinner. I need to buy three onions and two carrots. Also, I need to buy the beef and four potatoes. To finish, I need some oranges for the dessert.)

Exercise WR 2.2

1. Sí, ella tiene pelo largo. (No. She does not have long hair.)
2. Sí, ella es pelirroja. (Yes, she is a redhead.)
3. Él es bajo, fuerte y calvo. (He is short, strong, and bald.)
4. Él es bombero. (He is a firefighter.)
5. Ella es enfermera. (She is a nurse.)

Transcript:

Ricardo y Juana están en una fiesta. Están hablando de algunos miembros de sus familias que están allí también. (Ricardo and Juana are at a party. They are talking about some members of their families that are there as well.)

Hombre: Hola, Juana. ¿Dónde está tu hermana? (Hello, Juana. Where is your sister?)

Mujer: Hola, Ricardo. Mi hermana está allí. (Hello, Ricardo. My sister is over there.)

Hombre: ¿Dónde? (Where?)

Mujer: Es la mujer con pelo largo. (The woman with the long hair.)

Hombre: ¿Tiene pelo castaño? (Does she have brown hair?)

Mujer: No, es pelirroja. (No, she is a redhead.)

Hombre: Ah. ¿Es la mujer alta? (Oh, is she the tall woman?)

Mujer: ¡Sí! ¿Y dónde está tu padre? (Yes! And where is your father?)

Hombre: Mi padre está allí. Es el hombre bajo y fuerte. (My father is over there. He is the short, strong man.)

Mujer: ¿El hombre calvo? (The bald man?)

Hombre: Sí. Es calvo. (Yes. He's bald.)

Mujer: ¿Qué hace tu padre? (What does your father do?)

Hombre: Mi padre es bombero. ¿Qué hace tu hermana? (My father is a firefighter. What does your sister do?)

Mujer: Mi hermana es enfermera. (My sister is a nurse.)

Exercise WR 2.3

Sample: Yo soy baja. Yo soy trabajadora y divertida. Mi madre es baja también. Ella es simpática y tímida. Ella es oficinista. Yo soy estudiante. Somos de los Estados Unidos.

Exercise WR 2.4

Sample Answers:

1. Ahora mismo, estoy en casa. (Right now, I'm home.)
2. Sí, tengo hermanos. Tengo dos hermanos y una hermana. (Yes, I have siblings. I have two brothers and a sister.)
3. Ahora mismo estoy feliz. (Right now I am happy.)
4. Sí, soy muy habladora. (Yes, I am very talkative.)
5. Sí, soy extrovertida. (Yes, I am an extrovert.)

Exercise WR 2.5

1. Las chicas bajas / 2. El país grande / 3. Un perro feo / 4. Un gato gordo / 5. Unos hombre débiles / 6. El profesor aburrido / 7. La casa amarilla

Exercise WR 2.6

Set 1: a. I am an unhappy person.		b. I am unhappy right now.
Set 2: a. She is ready.		b. She is clever.
Set 3: a. We are bored.		b. We are boring.
Set 4: a. They are evil.		b. They are sick.

Exercise WR 2.7

1. Yo tengo pelo medio-largo. (I have medium-long hair.)
2. Nosotros somos de Inglaterra. (We are from England.)
3. Ellos tienen ojos marrones. (They have brown eyes.)
4. Mi padre tiene bigote. (My father has a mustache.)
5. Tú eres muy alto. (You are very tall.)
6. Mis amigos son honestos. (My friends are honest.)
7. Ellas son valientes. (They are brave.)
8. Nosotros tenemos pelo rizado. (We have curly hair.)

Exercise WR 2.8

1. I have medium-length hair. / 2. We are from England. / 3. They have brown eyes. /4. My father has a mustache. / 5. You are very tall. / 6. My friends are honest. / 7. They are brave. / 8. We have curly hair.

Week 3, Day 1: More with *Estar*

What's in store for you today: The verb **estar**

Listen to Track 3.1.1

María: *Hola, Lucía. ¿Cómo estás hoy?* (Hello, Lucía. How are you today?)

Lucía: *Estoy despistada.* (I am distracted.)

María: *¿Por qué?* (Why?)

Lucía: *Estoy muy nerviosa porque tengo un examen mañana.* (I'm nervous because I have an exam tomorrow.)

María: *¿Estás lista para el examen?* (Are you ready for the test?)

Lucía: *No sé. Estoy agobiada y preocupada.* (I don't know. I am overwhelmed and worried.)

The Verb "*Estar*"

We've talked about *ser* and how it's used for permanent characteristics as well as a number of other things. Well, today, we're going to talk about the verb *estar*, which is used for temporary conditions (as well as a number of other things, too).

Before we dive in, though, let's review the conjugation we'll use for *estar*.

Listen to Track 3.1.2

Yo estoy (I am)	*Nosotros/as estamos* (We are)
Tú estás (You are)	*Vosotros/as estáis* (You are)
Él/Ella/Usted está (He / she / you are)	*Ellos/as/Ustedes están* (They are)

P.L.A.C.E

Like with "ser," we looked at an acronym to help us remember when to use ***estar***. It was:

- **P**osition (The dog is next to the couch.)
- **L**ocation (I am in the store.)
- **A**ction (present progressive – we'll get to this later.)
- **C**ondition (I am tired.)
- **E**motion (I am happy.)

Today, we're going to work with **condition** and **emotion**. **Action** we will save for later. **Location** we'll look at tomorrow, as well as a little bit of **position**.

¿Estás agobiado? (Are you overwhelmed?)

Listen to Track 3.1.3

I certainly hope you're not feeling too ***agobiado*** right now. These last two weeks have been a lot of Spanish! Today, we're going to keep adding to it!

Here are some common emotions/states in Spanish:

Enfadado/a- – Mad/Angry	***Preocupado/a*** – Worried
Avergonzado/a – Embarrassed	***Enfermo/a*** – Sick
Ocupado/a – Busy	***De buen humor*** – In a good mood
Confundido/a – Confused	***De mal humor*** – In a bad mood
Emocionado/a – Excited	***Tranquilo/a*** – Calm
Nervioso/a – Nervous	***Asustado/a*** – Scared
Agobiado/a – Overwhelmed	***Despistado/a*** – Distracted/Lost in thought/Absent-minded
Relajado/a – Relaxed	
Cansado/a – Tired	

Exercise 3.1.1

Answer the following questions using the new vocabulary we looked at today and the verb *estar*.

¿Cómo te sientes cuando estás en una fiesta muy grande? (How do you feel when you are at a very big party?)

En una fiesta grande (in a big party) _______________________________________

¿Cómo te sientes en el trabajo? (How do you feel at work?)

En el trabajo (at work) _______________________________________

¿Cómo te sientes al llegar a casa después de un día largo? (How do you feel when you get home after a long day?)

Después de un día largo (after a long day) _______________________________

¿Cómo te sientes cuando estás con tus amigos? (How do you feel when you are with your friends?)

Cuando estoy con mis amigos (when I'm with my friends) ___________________

¿Cómo te sientes antes de un examen muy importante? (How do you feel when you are with your friends?)

Antes de un examen muy importante (before an important test) _____________

Estoy... Estás...Está...

Listen to Track 3.1.4

Let's take a moment to talk a little bit more about conjugating verbs. Although it may seem a little overwhelming remembering all those different verb forms, the truth is, it's an integral and useful part of Spanish.

One of the things that makes it so useful is that by conjugating the verb, we have the option to omit the subject in many cases:

- *Estoy en casa.* (I'm at home.)
- *Estás de mal humor.* (You're in a bad mood.)
- *Estamos asustados.* (We are scared.)

Our 3rd person conjugations can even drop the subject if we're sure that everyone we're talking to knows who exactly we're talking about:

- *Mi hermano está cansado. Está enfermo.* (My brother is tired. [He] is sick.)

Up until now, we've been keeping our subject pronouns in our sentences. This has been so that we can be sure that we learn them. But, going forward, if you're feeling confident, go ahead and drop them if the situation allows it!

Exercise 3.1.2

Let's just check our vocabulary knowledge. Match these words with their English equivalents:

1.	*Tranquilo/a*	a.	Confused
2.	*De mal humor*	b.	Scared
3.	*Enfadado/a*	c.	Relaxed
4.	*Emocionado/a*	d.	Calm
5.	*Despistado/a*	e.	Excited
6.	*Nervioso/a*	f.	Busy
7.	*Avergonzado/a*	g.	Overwhelmed
8.	*Relajado/a*	h.	In a good mood
9.	*Preocupado/a*	i.	Absent-minded/Distracted/Lost in thought
10.	*Enfermo/a*	j.	Tired
11.	*Ocupado/a*	k.	In a bad mood
12.	*Cansado/a*	l.	Sick
13.	*Confundido/a*	m.	Nervous
14.	*Agobiado/a*	n.	Embarrassed
15.	*De buen humor*	o.	Worried
16.	*Asustado/a*	p.	Angry

Practice Corner

Listening:

Listen to Track 3.1.5

Exercise 3.1.3

Listen to the track and put the sentences in order:

- *está---de---mi---mal---ahora--amigo---humor* - ___________________
- *muy---nosotros----agobiados---estamos* - ___________________
- *estás---asustada---poco---un* - ___________________
- *avergonzada---estoy---bastante* - ___________________

Writing:

Exercise 3.1.4

Write about your current condition/state and about that of one of your friends or family members.

____

____

____

Grammar:

Exercise 3.1.5

Each of these sentences contains one mistake. It could be conjugation or adjective agreement. Find and correct the mistakes:

1. *Nosotros estamos tranquilo.* - ___________________
2. *Mi amiga estás enferma.* - ___________________
3. *Ellas están cansados.* - ___________________
4. *Mis padres estamos avergonzados.* - ___________________
5. *Tú estoy de mal humor.* - ___________________

Vocabulary:

Exercise 3.1.6

Translate the following sentences from Spanish into English:

1. *Mi novia está preocupada.* - _______________________________________
2. *El contable está en su oficina.* - _______________________________________
3. *Tú estás despistado.* - _______________________________________
4. *Nosotros estamos enfadados.* - _______________________________________
5. *Los vendedores están de buen humor.* - _______________________________________

A Quick Recap of this Lesson

Today, we talked about using *estar* with emotions and conditions.

- We learned some new vocabulary to use with these situations.
- We also talked about one of the benefits of conjugating verbs - the subject pronouns become optional!

ANSWERS:

Exercise 3.1.1

Sample answers:

- En una fiesta grande estoy emocionada. (At a big party I am excited.)
- En el trabajo, estoy aburrida y de mal humor. (At work, I am bored and in a bad mood.)
- Después de un día largo, estoy cansada. (After a long day, I am tired.)
- Cuando estoy con mis amigos, estoy de buen humor. (When I am with my friends, I am in a good mood.)
- Antes de un examen muy importante, estoy nerviosa y preocupada. (Before a very important exam, I am nervous and worried.)

Exercise 3.1.2

1. D (Calm)
2. K (In a bad mood)
3. P (Angry)
4. E (Excited)
5. I (Absent-minded/ Distracted/Lost in thought)
6. M (Nervous)
7. N (Embarrassed)
8. C (Relaxed)
9. (Worried)
10. L (Sick)
11. F (Busy)
12. J (Tired)
13. A (Confused)
14. G (Overwhelmed)
15. H (In a good mood)
16. B (Scared)

Exercise 3.1.3

Mi amigo está de mal humor ahora. (My friend is in a bad mood now.)
Nosotros estamos muy agobiados. (We are very overwhelmed.)

Estás un poco asustada. (You are a little afraid.)

Estoy bastante avergonzada. (I am pretty embarrassed.)

Exercise 3.1.4

Example:

Estoy en el salón. Estoy relajada y de buen humor. Mi marido está en la oficina. Él está ocupado.

(I am in the living room. I am relaxed and in a good mood. My husband is in the office. He is busy.)

Exercise 3.1.5

1. Nosotros estamos tranquilos. (We are calm.)
2. Mi amiga está enferma. (My friend is sick.)
3. Ellas están cansadas. (They are tired.)
4. Mis padres están avergonzados. (My parents are ashamed.)
5. Tú estás de mal humor. (You are in a bad mood.)

Exercise 3.1.6

1. My girlfriend is worried.
2. The accountant is in his office.
3. You are distracted.
4. We are angry.
5. The salespeople are in a good mood.

Week 3, Day 2: More with *Estar* and Question Words

What's in store for you today: More with **estar**, and question words

Listen to Track 3.2.1

Man: *Hola, María. ¿Dónde estás?* (Hello, Maria. Where are you?)

Woman: *Hola, Diego. Todavía estoy en casa. ¿Dónde estás tú?* (Hello Diego. I am still at home. Where are you?)

Man: *Estoy en el bar. Juan y Andrea están conmigo.* (I'm at the bar. Juan and Andrea are with me)

Woman: *Llego en cinco minutos.* (I will be there in five minutes.)

Man: *Vale. Esperamos en la puerta.* (Okay. We wait at the door.)

Woman: *Gracias. ¡Hasta luego!* (Thanks. Bye!)

Man: *Adiós. ¡Hasta luego!* (Thanks. Bye!)

Yesterday, we looked at using *estar* to talk about emotions and states (**Estoy enfadado. Estás despistado.** - I am angry. You're clueless) Today, let's look at using *estar* to talk about location!

¿Dónde estás?

Listen to Track 3.2.2

Let's take a moment to look at some useful vocabulary for talking about location:

- **En la ciudad** (In the city):
  o **La biblioteca** – The library
  o **El hotel** – The hotel
  o **El banco** – The bank
  o **El supermercado** – The grocery store
  o **El hospital** – The hospital
  o **La tienda** – The store
  o **El restaurante** – The restaurant
  o **La farmacia** – The pharmacy
  o **En casa** – In the house/At home
  o **El parque** – The park

- **Las preposiciones** (The prepositions):
  o **En** – In/At/On
  o **Al lado de** – Next to
  o **A la derecha de** – To the right of
  o **A la izquierda de** – To the left of
  o **Cerca de** – Close to
  o **Delante de** – In front of
  o **Detrás de** – Behind
  o **Entre** – Between

You might notice that a lot of those "**place**" vocabulary words look a lot like their English equivalents (**we've seen this before with professions, as well**). These words are called "cognates." They are words that are similar in two (or three, or four...) different languages.

These words are handy because you'll find that you actually know a lot more Spanish than you thought, just because you speak English. Be careful, though! There are some things called "false cognates." These are words that <u>are not</u> what they seem.

Up to now, we haven't come across any of those evil little false cognates. But when we do, we'll be sure to point them out so you can give them a little extra practice.

Exercise 3.2.1

Listen to Track 3.2.3

Listen as the speaker says where different places are located in his city. Look at the map and decide if what he says is true (***verdad***) or false (***falso***) and correct the false statements.

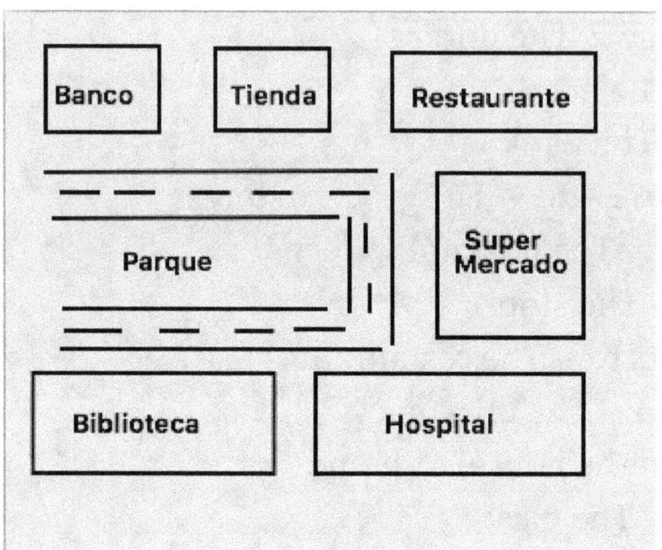

- *El parque está delante de la tienda. -* _______________________________
- *El restaurante está al lado del hospital. -* _______________________________
- *La biblioteca está a la derecha del hospital. -* _______________________________
- *El supermercado está detrás del hospital. -* _______________________________
- *El banco está cerca del parque. -* _______________________________
- *La tienda está entre el restaurante y el hospital. -* _______________________________

Something to note:

Listen to Track 3.2.4

We discussed contractions before when we were talking about where we're from (***Soy del Reino Unido***). You'll notice them here as well.

- Whenever you have the preposition ***de*** followed by the article ***el***, you can mush them together to create one word: ***del***.

- We will use another contraction (the only other one in Spanish, by the way) when we're talking about locations: **al**
  - **Al** is formed when we combine the preposition **a** (to) with the article **el**.

Asking Questions:

Listen to Track 3.2.5

In Spanish, there are a couple of ways to go about asking questions. A lot of it will depend on your intonation. For example, the question, "**Are you from Spain?**" can be asked:

- Example 1: **¿Es usted de España?**
- Example 2: **¿Usted es de España?**
- Example 3: **Usted es de España, ¿no?**
- Example 4: **Usted es de España, ¿verdad?**

Generally speaking, asking questions in Spanish is a lot like asking questions in English. You can change the order of the words (put the verb first – Example 1). You can do all the work with your voice (i.e. your intonation – Example 2). Or you can add a "question tag" (like in Examples 3 and 4).

Listen to Track 3.2.6

Yet another way to ask a question, like in English, is with a question word. Below you'll find the most common question words in Spanish:

1. **¿Qué?** – What?
2. **¿Dónde?** – Where?
3. **¿Por qué?** – Why?
4. **¿Quién?** – Who(m)?
5. **¿Cuándo?** – When?
6. **¿Cuánto?** – How much?/How many?

Exercise 3.2.2

Fill in the blanks below using either **ser** or **estar**.

1. *¿Quién _________ el Presidente de España?* (Who is the president of Spain?)
2. *¿Dónde _____________ mi hermano?* (Where is my brother?)
3. *¿Cuánta* gente _____________ aquí ahora?* (How many people are here now?)

4. *¿Cuándo* ______________ *la reunión?* (When is the meeting?)

5. *¿Por qué* ______________ *triste?* (Why are you sad?)

Listen to Track 3.2.7

> ***Note:** *"Cuanto"* can change from masculine or feminine and singular to plural depending on what is being asked about.

- ***¿Cuántas niñas hay en la escuela?*** (How many girls are there in the school) – Here, we're talking about a group of girls, so we use the feminine plural.

- ***¿Cuántos niños hay en la escuela?*** (How many children are there in the school?) – Here, we're talking about a group of children (may be only boys, may be boys and girls. Remember, when there's a mixed group of males and females, the masculine form is used - like we saw with *"nosotros"* and *"ellos"*).

Listen to Track 3.2.8

When **cuánto** is followed by a verb, it won't change.

- ***¿Cuánto cuesta?*** (How much does it cost?)
- ***¿Cuánto quieres?*** (How much do you want?)

Practice Corner

Exercise 3.2.3

Listen to Track 3.2.9

Listen to the conversation and answer the questions (try to answer in complete sentences!):

- *¿Dónde está María?* (Where is Maria?) - ________________________________
- *¿Dónde está Juan?* (Where's Juan?) - ________________________________
- *¿Dónde está la biblioteca?* (Where is the library?) - ________________________

Writing:

Exercise 3.2.4

Write a description of this town.

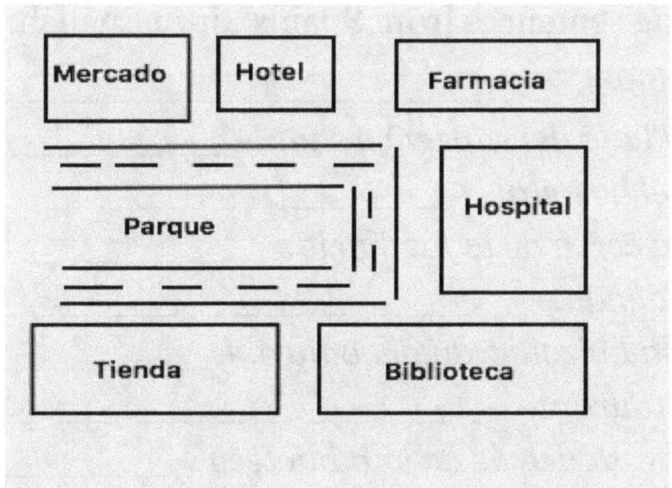

1. El hospital _____________ de la farmacia.
2. El hospital _________ de la biblioteca.
3. La tienda_________ de la biblioteca.
4. El hotel _________ del parque.
5. El hotel _________ el _____________ y la farmacia.
6. La biblioteca _______ a la ________ de la tienda.

Grammar:

Exercise 3.2.5

Fill in the blanks with the correct conjugations of *estar*.

1. *Yo* ___________ *en casa.* (I __________ at home.)
2. *Tú* __________ *en el restaurante.* (You __________ in the restaurant.)
3. *Nosotros* ___________ *en la tienda.* (We __________ in the store.)
4. *Él* ___________ *en la farmacia.* (He ___________ in the farmacy.)
5. *Ellos* __________ *en el hotel.* (They ___________ at the hotel.)
6. *Vosotros* __________ *en el supermercado.* (You _________ in the supermarket.)

Vocabulary:

Exercise 3.2.6

Translate the following sentences from Spanish into English.

1. *Estamos en el hotel.* - _______________________________________
2. *El hotel está al lado del supermercado.* - _______________________
3. *Ellos están en el hospital.* - _______________________________
4. *El hospital está cerca de la farmacia.* - _____________________
5. *Tú estás en la tienda.* - ___________________________________
6. *La tienda está a la izquierda del banco.* - ___________________
7. *Estoy en el restaurante.* - _________________________________
8. *El restaurante está detrás de la biblioteca.* - ________________

Exercise 3.2.7

Match the question words in Spanish with their English equivalents.

1. *¿Cuánto?*	a.	Why?
2. *¿Qué?*	b.	What?
3. *¿Por qué?*	c.	Where?
4. *¿Dónde?*	d.	How much?
5. *¿Quién?*	e.	When?
6. *¿Cuándo?*	f.	Who(m)?

A Quick Recap of this Lesson

Today, we talked about using *estar* with locations.

- We learned some vocabulary for "Around the city."
- And we learned some prepositions to give more specific locations.

We also talked about asking questions with question words. We learned:

¿Qué? – What?

¿Dónde? – Where?

¿Por qué? – Why?

¿Quién? – Who(m)?

¿Cuándo? – When?

¿Cuánto? – How much?/How many?

ANSWERS:

Exercise 3.2.1

1. The park is in front of the store: Verdad
2. The restaurant is next to the hospital.: Falso – El supermercado está al lado del hospital. OR El restaurante está al lado de la tienda. (The supermarket is next to the hospital. OR The restaurant is next to the store.)
3. The library is to the right of the hospital.: Falso – La biblioteca está a la izquierda del hospital. (The library is to the left of the hospital)
4. The supermarket is behind the hospital.: Verdad.
5. The bank is near the park.: Verdad.
6. The store is between the restaurant and the hospital.: Falso – La tienda está entre el banco y el restaurante. (The store is between the bank and the restaurant.)

Exercise 3.2.2

1. Es (asking about a profession)
2. Está (asking about location)

3. Está (asking about the number of people situated in a place)
4. Es (asking about time/date)
5. Estás (asking about a condition or state)

Exercise 3.2.3

- María está en la tienda. (Maria is in the store.)
- Juan está en la biblioteca. (Juan is in the library.)
- La biblioteca está cerca al parque, entre el hotel y la farmacia. (The library is near the park. It is between the hotel and the pharmacy.)

Transcript:

Juan: Hola, María. ¿Dónde estás? (Hello, María. Where are you?)

María: Hola, Juan. Estoy en la tienda. ¿Dónde estás tú? (Hello, Juan. I'm at the store. Where are you?)

Juan: Estoy en la biblioteca. (I'm in the library.)

María: ¿Dónde está la biblioteca? (Where is the library?)

Juan: Está cerca del parque. (It's close to the park.)

María: ¿Al lado del hospital? (Next to the hospital?)

Juan: No. No está cerca del hospital. Está a la derecha de hotel. (No. It's not near the hospital. It's to the right of the hotel.)

María: Ah. ¿Entre el hotel y la farmacia? (Ah. Between the hotel and the pharmacy?)

Juan: Sí. Está entre el hotel y la farmacia. (Yes. It's between the hotel and the pharmacy.)

Exercise 3.2.4

Suggested answers:

1. El hospital está delante de la farmacia. (The hospital is in front of the pharmacy.)
2. El hospital está detrás de la biblioteca. (The hospital is behind the library.)
3. La tienda está al lado de la biblioteca. (The store is next to the library.)
4. El hotel está detrás del parque. (The hotel is behind the park.)
5. El hotel está entre el supermercado y la farmacia. (The hotel is between the grocery store and the pharmacy.)
6. La biblioteca está a la derecha de la tienda. (The library is to the right of the store.)

Exercise 3.2.5:

1. Estoy (I am)
2. Estás (You are)
3. Estamos (We are)
4. Está (You are)
5. Están (You are)
6. Estáis (You are)

Exercise 3.2.6

1. We are in the hotel.
2. The hotel is next to the supermarket.
3. They are in the hospital.
4. The hospital is close to the pharmacy.
5. You are in the store.
6. The store is to the left of the bank.
7. I am in the restaurant.
8. The restaurant is behind the library.

Exercise 3.2.7

1. D (How much?), 2. B (What?), 3. A (Why?), 4. C (Where?), 5. F (Who[m]?), 6. E (When?)

Week 3, Day 3: Possessives in Spanish

What's in store for you today: Learning about possessives and talking about extended family

> **Today's goals are:**
>
> - To learn about the possessive in Spanish and possessive adjectives
> - To learn vocabulary for the extended family

Listen to Track 3.3.1

Juan: _María, ¿dónde está tu primo?_ (María, where is your cousin?)

María: _Mi primo está en casa. Está malo._ (My cousin is at home. He is sick.)

Juan: _¡Oh no! ¿Y tu tía?_ (Oh no! And your aunt?)

María: _Ella está en la tienda. Está preocupada._ (She is at the store. She's worried.)

Juan: _Tiene sentido. Su hijo está enfermo._ (That makes sense. Her son is sick.)

María: _Sí. Ella es una persona muy simpática. Le cuida muy bien._ (Yes. She is a very nice person. She takes good care of him.)

Today, we're going to talk about the possessive in Spanish (**my, your, his, etc.**). In addition, we're going to look at how to say things like "**María's cousin**" or "**María's aunt.**"

Listen to Track 3.3.2

La madre de mi amigo... My friend's mother (OR _La casa de mi amigo_... My friend's house)

This may seem like a long way to say a short phrase, but this is exactly how it's said in Spanish!

Listen to Track 3.3.3

In Spanish, there is no apostrophe ('). Instead, we use the preposition *de* (of) when we want to make something possessive.

- *El padre de mi novio* (The father of my boyfriend – my boyfriend's father)
- *La casa de mi amigo* (The house of my friend – my friend's house)
- *El bolígrafo de Juan* (The pen of Juan – Juan's pen)
- *La tienda del padre de María* (The store of the father of María – Maria's father's store)

It's not overly complicated. But it does take a little bit of a thought shift. You will say what is being possessed first, then the preposition *de*, then the person or thing that possesses it.

- *El libro de María* (the book of María)
- *El escritorio de Pablo* (the desk of Pablo)
- *La novia de mi amigo* (the girlfriend of my friend)
- *La madre de Juan* (the mother of Juan)

Exercise 3.3.1

Write out the following in Spanish:

1. María's mom - _______________________________
2. My friend's dog - _______________________________
3. My brother's cat - _______________________________
4. The doctor's office - _______________________________
5. Juan's job - _______________________________

Mi, Tu, Su...

Just like in English, we have another option for showing possession. We don't always use the apostrophe ('). Sometimes, we use possessive adjectives.

Listen to Track 3.3.4

Below, you'll find the possessive adjectives in Spanish. You're probably already familiar with the first one!

Mi/ Mis- My	**Nuestro/a/os/as**- Our
Tu/ Tus- Your (singular –informal)	**Vuestro/a/os/as**- Your (plural – informal)
Su/ Sus- His/Her/Its/Your (singular – formal)	**Su/ Sus**- Their/Your (plural – formal)

You'll notice that we're still using our handy little chart so you know exactly which person will take which possessive adjective.

Rules to Remember:

Listen to Track 3.3.5

Like with everything else in Spanish, our possessive adjectives have to AGREE AGREE.

- Your adjectives will describe <u>the thing being possessed.</u> NOT the possessor.
  - This means if you have two pens, your adjective will be plural:
    - *Mi bolígrafo* (My pen)
    - *Mis bolígrafos* (My pens)
  - Here are some more examples:
    - *Mi amigo necesita su libro.* (My friend needs his book.)
    - *Mi amigo necesita sus libros.* (My friend needs his books.)
    - *Tus padres están muy enfadados.* (Your parents are very angry.)
    - *Mi hermano está en su habitación.* (My brother is in his room.)
    - *Su familia tiene dos casas. ¡Sus casas son muy grandes!* (His/her/their family has two houses. His/her/their houses are very big!)
  - You'll notice that with *su*, the translations can mean a couple of different things. The context will let you know which subject you're talking about.

Listen to Track 3.3.6

- ### _Nuestro/a/os/as_ and _Vuestro/a/os/as_
  - These two possessive adjectives will change not only between singular and plural, but also between masculine and feminine. STILL it's what's being possessed that determines what form these adjectives will take:
    - _¿Dónde está nuestro libro?_ (Where is our book?)
    - _¿Dónde están nuestros libros?_ (Where are our books?)
    - _Nuestra escuela está cerca del parque._ (Our school is near the park.)
    - _Vuestro profesor es muy simpático._ (Your – plural, familiar – teacher is very nice.)
    - _Vuestras clases son interesantes_ (Your – plural, familiar – classes are interesting.)

Exercise 3.3.2

Translate the following sentences from Spanish into English:

1. _Mis hermanos son altos._ - _______________________________________
2. _Nuestra casa está cerca del restaurante._ - _______________________________
3. _Sus padres son simpáticos._ - _______________________________________
4. _Mi amiga tiene pelo castaño. Su pelo es largo._ - _______________________
5. _Tengo tres hermanos. ¡Sus habitaciones siempre (always) están sucias!_

   ____

Vocabulary: The Family

Let's take some time now to grow our vocabulary, shall we?

One of the things a lot of people talk about with some frequency is their family. So let's look at the vocabulary we need to be able to chat about ours in Spanish!

Listen to Track 3.3.7

- **Madre** – Mother
- **Padre** – Father
- **Hijo/a** – Son/Daughter
- **Hermano/a** – Brother/Sister
- **Tío** – Uncle
- **Tía** – Aunt

- **Primo/a** – Cousin
- **Abuelo** – Grandfather
- **Abuela** – Grandmother
- **Sobrino/a** – Nephew/Niece
- **Nieto/a** – Grandson/Granddaughter
- **Marido/ Mujer** – Husband/Wife (used in Spain)
- **Esposo/Esposa** – Husband/Wife (used in Latin America)

Like with "*padres*" and "*hermanos*" if we want to say, "I have four aunts and uncles" we'll use the masculine form: ***Tengo cuatro tíos.*** The same goes for grandparents, grandchildren, cousins, and nieces and nephews. ***Tengo cuatro sobrinos--dos sobrinas y dos sobrinos*** (I have four nieces and nephews – two nieces and two nephews).

Listen to Track 3.3.8

Listen to the conversation and see how much of it you can understand. Listen for words you are familiar with and for some of the new words we've just discussed.

Juan: *Hola, María. ¿Quiénes son tus amigos?* (Hello, María. Who are your friends?)

María: *Hola, Juan. Él es mi hermano, Miguel. Y ella es mi prima, Rosa.* (Hello, Juan. He is my brother, Miguel. And she is my cousin, Rosa.)

Juan: *Hola, Miguel. Hola, Rosa. Es un placer conocerles.* (Hello, Miguel. Hello, Rosa. It's a pleasure to meet you.)

Rosa: *Encantada.* (Pleased to meet you.)

Miguel: *Encantado.* (Pleased to meet you.)

Exercise 3.3.3

Look at the family tree below and answer the questions:

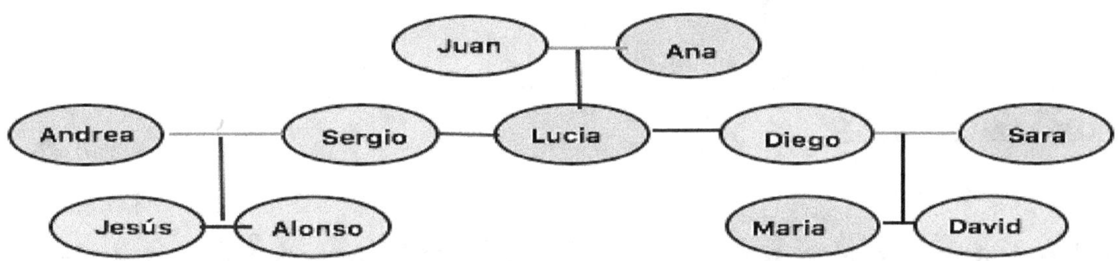

> **Note:** Pink lines equal relation through marriage. Black lines show biological relation. (i.e. Sergio, Lucía, and Diego are all siblings, and Diego and Sara are married).

1. *¿Quién es la madre de Lucia?* (Who is Lucia's mother?) - ___________________
2. *¿Quién es el hijo de Diego?* (Who is Diego's son?) - _____________________
3. *¿Quién es la mujer (la esposa) de Juan?* (Who is Juan's wife?) - ____________
4. *¿Quién es la prima de Alonso?* (Who is Alonso's female cousin?) - _________
5. *¿Quién es la sobrina de Lucia?* (Who is Lucia's niece?) - __________________
6. *¿Quién es el hermano de Jesús?* (Who is Jesús' brother?) - ________________
7. *¿Quién es el abuelo de David?* (Who is David's grandfather?) - ___________

Practice Corner

Listening:

Listen to Track 3.3.9

Exercise 3.3.4

Listen to the track and answer the questions (try to answer in complete sentences!):

- *¿Cuántos hermanos tiene Alejandra?* (How many siblings does Alejandra have?)

  ____

- *¿Cómo son sus hermanas?* (What are her sisters like?)

  ____

- *¿Cómo es su hermano?* (What is her brother like?)

  ____

- *¿Cuántos hijos tiene su tía Juana?* (How many children does her aunt Juana have?)

  ____

- *¿Cómo son los primos de Alejandra?* (What are Alejandra's cousins like?)

  ____

- *¿Dónde está la casa de su tío Marco?* (Where is her uncle Marco's house?)

  ____

- *¿Dónde está la casa de su tío Jorge?* (Where is her uncle Jorge's house?)

  ____

Writing:

Exercise 3.3.5

Write a description of your family. Use as much of the vocabulary you have learned as possible. Talk about what they are like, what they do (professions) and, of course, don't forget to use your possessives!

____

Vocabulary and Grammar:

Exercise 3.3.6

Translate the following sentences from Spanish into English:

1. *Su escritorio está entre el escritorio de Juan y el escritorio de María.*

2. *La farmacia de mi sobrino está a la izquierda del restaurante.*

3. *Mi amiga tiene cuatro primos. Sus primos son jóvenes.*

4. *Mis abuelos son viejos, son divertidos.*

5. *Nuestra casa está cerca de la tienda de Juan.*

6. *Gloria tiene dos nietos. Sus nietos son lindos.*

A Quick Recap of this Lesson

Today, we talked about possessives in Spanish.

- We mentioned that the apostrophe (') doesn't exist in Spanish. Instead, we use the preposition **de**.
- We also talked about the possessive adjectives:

Mi/ Mis- My	**Nuestro/a/os/as**- Our
Tu/ Tus- Your (singular – familiar)	**Vuestro/a/os/as**- Your (plural – familiar)
Su/ Sus- His/Her/Its/Your (singular – formal)	**Su/ Sus**- Their/Your (plural – formal)

We discussed how they need to agree with the noun they are describing in number and gender (for the 1st and 2nd person plural).

We also looked at vocabulary for the extended family.

ANSWERS:

Exercise 3.3.1

1. La madre de María
2. El perro de mi amigo
3. El gato de mi hermano
4. La oficina del médico
5. El trabajo de Juan

Exercise 3.3.2

1. My brothers are tall.
2. Our house is close to the restaurant.
3. His/Her/Their parents are nice.
4. My friend has brown hair. Her hair is long.
5. I have three brothers. Their rooms are always dirty!

Exercise 3.3.3

1. Ana es la madre de Lucia (Ana is Lucia's mother)
2. David es el hijo de Diego. (David is Diego's son.)

3. Ana es la mujer (esposa) de Juan. (Ana is Juan's wife (spouse).)
4. Maria es la prima de Alonso. (Maria is Alonso's cousin.)
5. Maria es la sobrina de Lucía (Maria is Lucia's niece)
6. Alonso es el hermano de Jesús. (Alonso is the brother of Jesus.)
7. Juan es el abuelo de David. (Juan is David's grandfather.)

Exercise 3.3.4

- Alejandra tiene tres hermanos. (Alejandra has three brothers.)
- Sus hermanas son extrovertidas. (Her sisters are outgoing.)
- Su hermano es tímido. (Her brother is shy.)
- Su tía Juana tiene tres hijos. (Her aunt Juana has three children.)
- Sus primos son divertidos. (Their cousins are fun.)
- La casa de su tío Marco está cerca de su oficina. (His uncle Marco's house is near his office.)
- La casa de su tío Jorge está al lado del hospital. (Her uncle Jorge's house is next to the hospital.)

Transcript:

Hola, soy Alejandra. Tengo una familia grande. Tengo tres hermanos--dos hermanas y un hermano. Mis hermanas son extrovertidas. Mi hermano es tímido. Tengo tres tíos. Mi tía Juana tiene tres hijos. Son mis primos. Mis primos son divertidos. Sus padres son profesores. Mi tío Marco es dentista. Su casa está cerca de su oficina. Mi tío Jorge es enfermero. Su casa está al lado del hospital.

(Hello, I'm Alejandra. I have a big family. I have three siblings – two sisters and one brother. My sisters are outgoing. My brother is shy. I have three aunts and uncles. My aunt Juana has three children. They are my cousins. My cousins are fun. Their parents are teachers. My uncle Marco is a dentist. His house is close to his office. My uncle Jorge is a nurse. His house is next to the hospital.)

Exercise 3.3.5

Sample answer:

Mis padres viven en Chicago. Mi hermano vive en Chicago, también. Él es contable. Mi hermano tiene cuatro hijos--dos hijos y una hija. Mis sobrinos son jóvenes. Mi sobrina Amanda es pelirroja y mi sobrina Jennifer tiene pelo largo. Mis sobrinos tienen pelo corto. También, tengo una hermana. Ella es oficinista y su marido es fontanero. Ellos tiene un hijo. Mi sobrino es alto y fuerte. Ellos viven en Denver.

(My parents live in Chicago. My brother lives in Chicago, too. He is an accountant. My brother has four children - two sons and one daughter. My nephews are young. My niece Amanda is a redhead and my niece Jennifer has long hair. My nephews have short hair. Also, I have a sister. She is an office worker and her husband is a plumber. They have a son. My nephew is tall and strong. They live in Denver.)

Exercise 3.3.6

1. His/Her desk is between Juan's desk and María's desk.
2. My nephew's pharmacy is to the left of the restaurant.
3. My friend has four cousins. Her cousins are young.
4. My grandparents are old. But they are fun.
5. Our house is close to Juan's store.
6. Gloria has two grandchildren. Her grandchildren are beautiful.

Week 3, Day 4: -*AR* Verb Conjugations and More with Questions

What's in store for you today: -*AR* verbs

> **Today's goals are:**
>
> - To learn about the -*ar* conjugation
> - To learn more about asking questions

Listen to Track 3.4.1

Girl: *Yo estudio mucho. Estudio español todos los días. ¿Estudias tú español?* (I study a lot. I study Spanish every day. Do you study Spanish?)

Boy: *No, no estudio español. Pero mi amiga estudia español. Yo dibujo.* (No, I don't study Spanish. But my friend studies Spanish. I draw.)

Girl: *Yo no dibujo, pero mi padre dibuja muy bien.* (I don't draw, but my father draws very well.)

Boy: *¿Dibuja él todos los días?* (Does he draw everyday?)

Girl: *Sí, él dibuja todos los días.* (Yes, he draws everyday.)

Boy: *También, yo nado mucho. ¿Nadas tú?* (Also, I swim a lot. Do you swim?)

Girl: *¡Sí! Mis amigos y yo nadamos mucho.* (Yes! My friends and I swim a lot.)

Over the last two and a half weeks, we've learned a lot! By now, you understand subject pronouns, *ser* and *estar*, and can put together some pretty complex sentences. Today, we're going to start working on a very important part of Spanish that will help to significantly grow your ability to use the language. We're going to start looking at verbs!

-Ar Verbs

Listen to Track 3.4.2

The verbs we've looked at before (*ser*, *estar*, and *tener*) are considered <u>irregular</u> verbs. This means that they don't follow the traditional verb conjugation patterns that others do. Let's start getting familiar with those patterns. Today, we're going to work with the first group of verbs: the *-ar* verbs.

Some of the most common regular *-ar* verbs are:

1. **Hablar** – To talk
2. **Caminar** – To walk
3. **Trabajar** – To work
4. **Estudiar** – To study
5. **Escuchar** – To listen
6. **Visitar** – To visit
7. **Viajar** – To travel
8. **Usar** – To use
9. **Llegar** – To arrive
10. **Bailar** – To dance
11. **Nadar** – To swim
12. **Cocinar** – To cook
13. **Llorar** – To cry
14. **Terminar** – To finish
15. **Esperar** – To wait
16. **Buscar** – To search for
17. **Mirar** – To look (at)
18. **Pintar** – To paint
19. **Pagar** – To pay
20. **Comprar** – To buy
21. **Ayudar** – To help
22. **Necesitar** – To need
23. **Desayunar** – To have breakfast
24. **Cenar** – To have dinner
25. **Dejar** – To leave (i.e. To abandon)/To quit/To let

You'll notice that all of the verbs end in *-ar*, hence why they are called "*-ar* verbs." When you see a verb in this form (with the *-ar* ending still attached), it's called an <u>infinitive</u>. You'll also notice that the English translation of verbs that are in their infinitive form include the "to" before them ("to talk," "to help," etc.).

However, these verbs aren't going to keep that *-ar* around forever! We have to <u>conjugate</u> them.

Rules to Remember:

1. To conjugate your regular -*ar* verbs, you'll take off that -*ar* ending
2. and add one of the following, depending on what your subject is:

Listen to Track 3.4.3

Yo (I) *-o*	*Nosotros/as* (we) *-amos*
Tú (you - singular familiar) *-as*	*Vosotros/as* (you – plural familiar) *-áis*
Él (he) *Ella* (she) *Usted* (you – singular formal) *-a*	*Ellos/ as* (they) *Ustedes* (you – plural formal) *-an*

Again, we're going to keep using this nifty little chart. Here, you'll find all your endings paired neatly with their corresponding subjects.

Listen to Track 3.4.4

If we were to take the verb "***hablar***" (to talk) and put it into that chart, it would look like this:

Yo hablo (I speak)	*Nosotros/as hablamos* (We speak)
Tú hablas (You speak)	*Vosotros/as habláis* (You speak)
Él/ Ella/ Usted habla (He / She speaks / You speak)	*Ellos/as/ Ustedes hablan* (They speak)

Following our steps, it's:

1. Hablar (Drop the *-ar*).
2. Pick your ending (*-o, -as, -a, etc.*) and add it onto the stem (what's left, in this case ***habl***).

Listen to Track 3.4.5

It would be the same with the verb "***cantar***" (to sing).

Yo canto (I sing)	*Nosotros/as cantamos* (We sing)
Tú cantas (You sing)	*Vosotros/as cantáis* (You sing)
Él/ Ella/ Usted canta (He / she sings / you sings)	*Ellos/as/ Ustedes cantan* (They sing)

Exercise 3.4.1

Let's try on some conjugation for size! Fill in the charts below using the verbs given.

Bailar *(Take off your -ar for your stem = Bailar)*

Yo	*Nosotros/as*
Tú	*Vosotros/as*
Él/ Ella/ Usted	*Ellos/as/ Ustedes*

Ayudar

Yo	*Nosotros/as*
Tú	*Vosotros/as*
Él/ Ella/ Usted	*Ellos/as/ Ustedes*

Present Tense Verbs in Spanish

Before we get too far ahead of ourselves here, let's talk about what we're talking about! The conjugations we're looking at here are for the <u>present tense</u>. That means that we're talking about things that are happening now – in the moment.

Listen to Track 3.4.6

In English, we only use the simple present when we say things like "**I talk**," or "**she reads**," or "**they run**." But in Spanish, the present tense can be used to convey a larger variety of things. So, when I say, "***yo hablo***" in Spanish, I can be saying any one of the following:

- I talk.
- I am talking.
- I do talk.

The context of my sentence will let the listener know which one I mean. For example, if you were to ask me, "***¿Qué haces?***" (What are you doing?), I can answer, "***hablo con mi madre***" (I'm talking to my mom) if I am literally in the process of talking to her – I'm standing there, on the phone, in the middle of my conversation.

Listen to Track 3.4.7

Tengo una pregunta... I have a question...

Listen to Track 3.4.8

Yesterday, we talked about question words:

- *¿Dónde trabajas?* – Where do you work?
- *¿Quién baila bien?* – Who dances well?

Today, let's talk a little bit more about questions.

Questions with "do" or "does"

You'll notice in the first example above *(¿Dónde trabajas?)* that there might seem like there's something missing! In English, we say, "where <u>do</u> you work?"

Listen to Track 3.4.9

In Spanish, "**do**" and "does" are <u>not</u> used in questions. Instead, we have a few options for how we're going to make questions, especially those that don't have a question word. For example:

- *¿Trabaja María en el restaurante?* (Does Maria work in the restaurant?)
- *¿María trabaja en el restaurante?* (Does Maria work at the restaurant?)

In the first example, we've switched the order of the words: Verb+subject. In the second, we have to use our voice and intonation to ensure that the people we're talking to know we're asking a question.

Exercise 3.4.2

Listen to Track 3.4.10

Using the following adverbs of frequency, answer the questions about yourself:

- *Siempre* – Always
- *A veces* – Sometimes
- *Nunca* – Never

> **Note:** For now, let's keep our adverbs of frequency <u>in front of the verb</u>.

Example: *Nunca nado. A veces bailo. Siempre cocino.*

Listen to Track 3.4.11

1. *¿Con qué frecuencia lloras?* (How often do you cry?)

   ____

2. *¿Con qué frecuencia estudias español?* (How often do you study Spanish?)

   ____

3. *¿Con qué frecuencia tocas el piano?* (How often do you play piano?)

   ____

4. *¿Con qué frecuencia llegas tarde al trabajo?* (How often do you arrive late to work?)

   ____

Practice Corner

Listening:

Listen to Track 3.4.12

Exercise 3.4.3

Listen to the sentences and put them in order:

- *muy---amigo---mi---cocina---bien* - _______________________________________
- *nunca--nosotros--bailamos---los---bares---en* - _______________________________
- *yo---a---con---amigos---ayudo---Español---mis---su* - _______________________
- *no---bien---cantan---ellos---muy* - ____
- *siempre---tú---viajas---nuevos--a---países* - ________________________________

Writing:

Exercise 3.4.4

Choose five of the verbs above and write sentences using them. Write about you, your friends, and your family.

____

____

____

____

Grammar:

Exercise 3.4.5

Conjugate the following verbs:

Llorar

Ayudar

Necesitar

Vocabulary:

Exercise 3.4.6

Match the verbs in Spanish with their English equivalents:

1. Escuchar	14. Terminar	a. To travel	n. To swim
2. Comprar	15. Trabajar	b. To help	o. To walk
3. Caminar	16. Viajar	c. To listen to	p. To leave/To quit
4. Estudiar	17. Hablar	d. To wait	q. To work
5. Pintar	18. Cenar	e. To buy	r. To look for
6. Llegar	19. Esperar	f. To arrive	s. To need
7. Visitar	20. Dejar	g. To have dinner	t. To study
8. Bailar	21. Buscar	h. To cry	u. To paint
9. Nadar	22. Necesitar	i. To visit	v. To finish
10. Desayunar	23. Pagar	j. To use	w. To pay
11. Usar	24. Mirar	k. To dance	x. To watch
12. Cocinar	25. Ayudar	l. To talk	y. To have breakfast
13. Llorar		m. To cook	

Additional Vocabulary:

Listen to Track 3.4.13

- ***Todos los días*** - Every day
- ***Con*** - With
- ***Mucho*** - A lot
- ***Poco*** - A little
- ***Bien*** - Well
- ***Muy*** - Very

A Quick Recap of this Lesson

Today, we talked about *-ar* verbs.

- We reviewed the conjugations for regular *-ar* verbs.
- We talked about dropping the infinitive verb ending, and adding the following to the stem:

Yo (I) **-o**	*Nosotros/as* (we) **-amos**
Tú (you – singular informal) **-as**	*Vosotros/as* (you – plural informal) **-áis**
Él (he) *Ella* (she) *Usted* (you – singular formal) **-a**	*Ellos/ as* (they) *Ustedes* (you – plural formal) **-an**

We also talked about the present tense in Spanish.

And, lastly, we looked at asking questions:

- There is no <u>do</u> or <u>does</u> in Spanish questions. Instead we:
  - Use our intonation OR
  - Use question tags OR
  - Change the order of the words.

ANSWERS:

Exercise 3.4.1

Bailar

Yo bailo (I dance)	Nosotros/as bailamos (We dance)
Tú bailas (You dance)	Vosotros/as bailan (You dance)
Él/ Ella/ Usted baila (He/She dances / You dance)	Ellos/as/ Ustedes bailan (They/You dance)

Ayudar

Yo ayudo (I help)	Nosotros/as ayudamos (We help)
Tú ayudas (I help)	Vosotros/as ayudan (You help)
Él/ Ella/ Usted ayuda (He/She helps / You help)	Ellos/as/ Ustedes ayudan (They/ You help)

Exercise 3.4.2

1. Siempre desayuno. (I always eat breakfast)
2. A veces lloro. (I sometimes cry)
3. A veces estudio español. (I sometimes study spanish)
4. Nunca toco el piano. (I never play the piano)
5. Siempre llego tarde al trabajo. (I always arrive late to work)

Exercise 3.4.3

- Mi amigo cocina muy bien. (My friend cooks very well.)
- Nosotros nunca bailamos en los bares. (We never dance in bars.)
- Yo ayudo a mis amigos con su español. (I help my friends with their Spanish.)
- Ellos no cantan muy bien. (They don't sing very well.)
- Tú siempre viajas a países nuevos. (You always travel to new countries.)

Exercise 3.4.4

Example:

Yo no nado bien. (I don't swim well.)

Mi amigo cocina muy bien. (My friend cooks very well.)

Mi padre trabaja en una tienda. (My father works in a store.)

Mis padres viajan mucho. (My parents travel a lot.)

Mis amigos y yo siempre bailamos. (My friends and I always dance.)

Exercise 3.4.5

Llorar

Yo lloro (I cry)	Nosotros/as lloran (We cry)
Tú lloras (You cry)	Vosotros/as lloran (You cry)
Él/ Ella/ Usted llora (He/She cries / You cry)	Ellos/as/ Ustedes lloran (They/You cry)

Ayudar

Yo ayudo (I help)	Nosotros/as ayudamos (We help)
Tú ayudas (You help)	Vosotros/as ayudan (You help)
Él/ Ella/ Usted ayuda (He/She helps / You help)	Ellos/as/ Ustedes ayudan (They/ You help)

Necesitar

Yo necesito (I need)	Nosotros/as necesitamos (We need)
Tú necesitas (You need)	Vosotros necesitan (You need)
Él/ Ella/ Usted necesita (He/She needs / You needs)	Ellos/as/ Ustedes necesitan (They/ You need)

Exercise 3.4.6

1. C (To listen to)
2. E (To buy)
3. (To walk)
4. T (To study)
5. U (To paint)
6. F (To arrive)
7. I (To visit)
8. K (To dance)
9. N (To swim)
10. Y (To have breakfast)
11. J (To use)
12. M (To cook)
13. H (To cry)
14. V (To finish)
15. Q (To work)
16. A (To travel)
17. L (To talk)
18. G (To have dinner)
19. D (To wait)
20. P (To leave/To quit)
21. R (To look for)
22. S (To need)
23. W (To pay)
24. X (To watch)
25. B (To help)

Week 3, Day 5: *-ER* and *-IR* Verb Conjugations

What's in store for you today: *-Er* and *-Ir* verbs:

Listen to Track 3.5.1

Juan: *Hola. Me llamo Juan. ¿Cómo te llamas?* (Hello, my name is Juan. What is your name?)

María: *Me llamo María. Encantada.* (My name is María. It's a pleasure.)

Juan: *Es un placer conocerte.* (It's a pleasure to meet you.)

María: *Yo vivo en Madrid. ¿Dónde vives tú?* (I live in Madrid. Where do you live?)

Juan: *Yo vivo en Ávila pero trabajo en Madrid.* (I live in Ávila but I work in Madrid.)

María: *¿Cómo llegas al trabajo?* (How do you get to work?)

Juan: *Uso el autobús. Leo en el viaje. ¿Lees mucho tú?* (I take the bus. I read during the journey. Do you read a lot?)

María: *Sí, leo mucho. También escribo. Mi hermano y yo escribimos un blog. ¿Escribes tú?* (Yes, I read a lot. Also, I write. My brother and I write a blog. Do you write?)

Juan: *No, no escribo.* (No, I don't write.)

Verb Conjugation Review

Last lesson we focused on *-ar* verb conjugations. In order to conjugate our verbs, we learned that you have to drop the ending from the infinitive (the *-ar* for *-ar* verbs) and add the appropriate ending.

In case you forgot, those looked like this:

-o	*-amos*
-as	*-áis*
-a	*-an*

We also mentioned that there are <u>three</u> categories for regular Spanish verbs. Today, let's look at the other two: *-er* and *-ir* verbs.

-Er Verbs

Listen to Track 3.5.2

Below you'll find a list of some of the most common *-er* verbs:

1. **Comer** – To eat
2. **Comprender** – To understand
3. **Correr** – To run
4. **Aprender** – To learn
5. **Responder** – To respond
6. **Vender** – To sell
7. **Depender** – To depend
8. **Proteger** – To protect
9. **Beber** – To drink
10. **Creer** – To believe
11. **Leer** – To read
12. **Romper** – To break
13. **Ver** – To see

So, we have all these verbs. Now what do we do with them? Conjugate them, of course! Don't forget to drop your *-er* ending before adding the conjugated ending.

The conjugations you will use for your *-er* verbs are:

-o	*-emos*
-es	*-éis*
e	*-en*

Listen to Track 3.5.3

So, the verb ***comer**** would be conjugated like this:

(Yo) como (I eat)	**(Nosotros/as) comemos** (We eat)
(Tú) comes (You eat)	**(Vosotros/as) coméis** (You eat)
(Él/Ella/Usted) come (He / She eats / You eat)	**(Ellos/as/Ustedes) comen** (They / you eat)

> ***Note:** *"Comer"* can mean **"to eat"** OR in Spain, it means **"to have lunch."**

Listen to Track 3.5.4

The verb ***ver*** is a little different than the others. But only in the 1st person singular and 2nd person plural. Here's how it conjugates:

Veo (I see)	**Vemos** (We see)
Ves (You see)	**Veis** (You see)
Ve (He/She sees /You see)	**Ven** (They/ You see)

Exercise 3.5.1

Conjugate the following verbs:

Comprender

Yo	*Nosotros/as*
Tú	*Vosotros/as*
Él/ Ella/ Usted	*Ellos/as/Ustedes*

Leer

Yo	*Nosotros/as*
Tú	*Vosotros/as*
Él/ Ella/ Usted	*Ellos/as/Ustedes*

-Ir Verbs

Listen to Track 3.5.5

Below you'll find a list of the most common regular *-ir* verbs:

1. **Abrir** – To open
2. **Decidir** – To decide
3. **Descubrir** – To discover
4. **Escribir** – To write
5. **Permitir** – To permit/To allow
6. **Recibir** – To receive
7. **Sufrir** – To suffer
8. **Subir** – To go up
9. **Vivir** – To live
10. **Asistir*** – To attend

* This is one of those tricky "false cognates" we talked about before. It might look like the word "assist" in English, but it's not! So be careful!

Our *-ir* conjugations will look like this:

-o	-imos
-es	-ís
-e	-en

You'll notice that most of these look very familiar! The only difference in the *-er* and *-ir* conjugations will be found in the 1st person plural and the 2nd person plural.

So, the verb ***abrir*** will look like this:

Listen to Track 3.5.6

Abro	Abrimos
Abres	Abrís
Abre	Abren

Exercise 3.5.2

Conjugate the following verbs:

Vivir

Yo	Nosotros/as
Tú	Vosotros/as
Él/ Ella/ Usted	Ellos/as/Ustedes

Escribir

Yo	*Nosotros/as*
Tú	*Vosotros/as*
Él/ Ella/ Usted	*Ellos/as/Ustedes*

Exercise 3.5.3

Listen to Track 3.5.7

Listen to the recording and fill in the blanks:

En mi trabajo, uso español con mucha frecuencia. _______________ un poco. _______________ correos electrónicos a mis cliente en México. También, _______________ en español.

The "Personal 'a'"

Listen to Track 3.5.8

Now that we have some verbs to play around with, we're probably going to want to start putting together some more complex sentences. That's great!

But before we do that, there's one little thing we need to discuss – the "personal '**a**'."

The personal '**a**' is used in Spanish when the object of the verb is a <u>person</u>. For example:

- ***Ayudo a mi madre con las tareas de casa***. (I help my mother with the housework.)
- ***Esteban escribe a sus abuelos cada semana***. (Esteban writes his grandparents every week.)
- ***Una madre protege a sus hijos***. (A mother protects her children.)

It is <u>required</u>. It is not optional. It may not seem natural now, but if you start making an effort to work it into your speech now, you'll find that, eventually, sentences sound weird without it.

Don't get this "**a**" confused with the preposition "**to**."

- ***Viajo a Miami con mucha frecuencia***. (I travel to Miami frequently.)

Practice Corner

Listening:

Listen to Track 3.5.9

Exercise 3.5.4

Listen to the track and answer the questions:

María está hablando de sus días. ¿Cómo son sus días?

1. *¿Qué NO hace María por las mañanas?* (What doesn't María do in the mornings?)
   a. *Trabajar* (Work)
   b. *Leer correos electrónicos* (Read emails)
   c. *Correr en el parque* (Run in the park)
   d. *Vender muchas cosas* (Sell a lot of things)

2. *¿Dónde come María?* (Where does María eat?)
   Answer with a complete sentence.

   ____

3. *¿Qué hace María por las tardes*? (What does María do in the afternoons?)
   a. Leer   b. Estudiar   c. Asistir a clases   d. Pintar

4. *¿Qué hace María por las noches?* (What does María do at night?)
   a. Leer   b. Estudiar   c. Asistir a clases   d. Pintar

Writing:

Exercise 3.5.5

Fill in the chart with the things you do at each time of the day (throw in some of the -*ar* verbs we used yesterday if you can!). Write a complete sentence (***yo leo un libro***; or just ***yo cocino***).

Por las mañanas **(In the mornings)**	***Por las tardes*** **(In the afternoons)**	***Por las noches*** **(At night)**

Grammar and Vocabulary:

Exercise 3.5.6

Fill in the blanks with the correct verbs (conjugated to the correct person):

- *Yo __________ (sufrir/ subir) las escaleras cada día.* (I _________ (suffer / climb) the stairs every day.)
- *Tú _________ (comprender/ creer) español.* (You _________ (understand / believe) Spanish.)
- *Mi hermana siempre __________ (decidir/ romper) mis cosas.* (IMy sister always__________ (decide/break) my stuff.)
- *Ellos no __________ (comer/ permitir) alcohol en su casa.* (They do not __________ (eat / allow) alcohol in their home.)
- *Nosotros __________ (abrir/ vender) la tienda a las 8:00.* (We__________ (open / sell) the store at 8:00.)

Exercise 3.5.7

Translate the following sentences from English into Spanish:

1. He discovers new things. - ___________________________________
2. You read, write, and understand Spanish. - ___________________________
3. They believe in ghosts. - ______________________________________
4. We drink a lot of coffee (café). - _________________________________
5. She sells laptops. - ____

A Quick Recap of this Lesson

Today we talked about the *-er* and *-ir* verb conjugations:

-er:

-o	*-emos*
-es	*-éis*
e	*-en*

-ir:

-o	*-imos*
-es	*-ís*
-e	*-en*

We also talked about using the "**personal 'a'**" when the object of a verb is a person:

Llamo a mi madre cada día. (I call my mother every day.)

ANSWERS:

Exercise 3.5.1

Comprender

Yo comprendo (I understand)	Nosotros/as comprendemos (We understand)
Tú comprendes (You understand)	Vosotros/as comprenden (You understand)
Él/ Ella/ Usted comprende (He/She understands / You understand)	Ellos/as/Ustedes comprenden (They/You understand)

Leer

Yo leo (I read)	Nosotros/as leemos (We read)
Tú lees (You read)	Vosotros/as leen (You read)
Él/ Ella/ Usted lee (He/She reads / You read)	Ellos/as/Ustedes leen (They/You read)

Exercise 3.5.2

Vivir

Yo vivo (I live)	Nosotros/as vivimos (We live)
Tú vives (You live)	Vosotros/as viven (You live)
Él/ Ella/ Usted vive (He/She lives / You live)	Ellos/as/Ustedes viven (They/You live)

Escribir

Yo escribo (I write)	Nosotros/as escribimos (We write)
Tú escribes (You write)	Vosotros/as escriben (You write)
Él/ Ella/ Usted escribe (He/She writes / You write)	Ellos/as/Ustedes escriben (They/You write)

Exercise 3.5.3

En mi trabajo, uso español con mucha frecuencia. Comprendo un poco. Escribo correos electrónicos a mis clientes en México. También, leo en español.

(In my job, I use Spanish a lot. I understand a little. I write emails to my clients in Mexico. Also, I read in Spanish.)

Exercise 3.5.4

1. C (correr en el parque)
2. María come en un restaurante cerca de su tienda.
3. C (asistir a clases de español)
4. A (leer)

Transcript:

Estoy muy ocupada. Por las mañanas, trabajo. En el trabajo, leo muchos correos electrónicos. Recibo muchos correos y respondo a muchas personas. También, vendo muchas cosas en mi tienda. Luego, como en un restaurante cerca de mi tienda. Por las tardes, corro en el parque con mi amiga. Corremos mucho. También, asisto a clases de español. Después, ceno en casa. Vivo al lado del parque. Por las noches, leo en la cama.

(I am very busy. In the mornings, I work. At work, I read a lot of emails. I receive a lot of emails and I reply to a lot of people. Also, I sell lots of things in my store. Then, I eat in a restaurant close to my store. In the afternoons, I run in the park with my friend. We run a lot. Also, I attend Spanish classes. Afterwards, I have dinner at home. I live next to the park. At night I read in bed.)

Exercise 3.5.5

Por las mañanas (In the mornings)	Por las tardes (In the afternoons)	Por las noches (At night)
Tomo café, leo el periódico. Yo trabajo y respondo correos. (I drink coffee, I read the paper. I work and respond emails)	Estudio español, ayudo a mi mamá en su casa. (I study spanish, I help my mom in her house)	Yo cocino la cena y leo un libro. (I cook dinner and read a book)

Exercise 3.5.6

- Subo
- Comprendes
- Rompe
- Permiten
- Abrimos

Exercise 3.5.7

1. Él descubre cosas nuevas.
2. Tú lees, escribes y comprendes español.
3. Ellos creen en los fantasmas.
4. Nosotros bebemos mucho café.
5. Ella vende portátiles.

Week 3 Recap

This week, we talked about *estar*, and learned how to conjugate our regular verbs. Let's take some time to review before we move on to Week 4!

Listening:

Listen to Track WR 3.1

Exercise WR 3.1

Listen to the track and answer the questions:

María y Juan están hablando por teléfono (María and Juan are talking on the phone):

1. *¿Dónde está María?* (Where is María?)
   a. *Está en casa* (She is at home.)
   b. *Está en el hospital* (She is at the hospital.)
   c. *Está en el trabajo* (She is at work.)
   d. *Está en el supermercado* (She is at the grocery store.)

2. *¿Dónde trabaja Juan?* (Where does Juan work?)
   a. *Trabaja al lado del hospital.* (He works next to the hospital.)
   b. *Trabaja cerca de la casa de María* (He works close to María's house.)
   c. *Trabaja en el restaurante* (He works in the restaurant.)
   d. *Trabaja en el hospital.* (He works at the hospital.)

3. *¿Qué van a hacer?* (What are they going to do?)
   a. *Comprar comida* (Buy food)
   b. *Trabajar juntos* (Work together)
   c. *Comer juntos* (Eat together)
   d. *Ir de compras* (Go shopping)

Listen to Track WR 3.2

Exercise WR 3.2

Listen to the track and answer the questions (answer with complete sentences):

María está hablando de su familia (María is talking about her family):

1. *¿Dónde viven los padres de María?* (Where do María's parents live?)

    ____

2. *¿Los padres de María venden mucha ropa?* (Do María's parents sell a lot of clothes?)

    ____

3. *¿Con quién asiste a la universidad?* (Who does María attend university with?)

    ____

4. *¿Dónde viven los abuelos de María?* (Where do María's grandparents live?)

    ____

Writing:

Exercise WR 3.3

Write a short paragraph talking about your family (immediate and extended). Where do they live? What do they do? What are they like?

Exercise WR 3.4

Contesta las preguntas. (Answer the questions.)

1. *¿Cómo te sientes cuando estás con tu familia?* (How do you feel when you're with your family?)

    ____

2. *¿Cómo te sientes cuando estás trabajando?* (How do you feel when you're working?)

    ____

3. *¿Cómo te sientes cuando estás con tus amigos?* (How do you feel when you're with your friends?)

    ____

4. *¿Cómo te sientes cuando estás de vacaciones?* (How do you feel when you're on vacation?)

    ____

5. *¿Cómo te sientes cuando tienes que madrugar?* (How do you feel when you have to wake up early?)

Grammar:

Exercise WR 3.5

Conjugate the following verbs:

Buscar (To look for)

Romper (To break)

Abrir (To open)

Vocabulary:

Exercise WR 3.6

Translate the following sentences from English into Spanish:

1. We are distracted today. - _______________________________________
2. What is she cooking? - _______________________________________
3. Why do you study Spanish? - _______________________________________
4. My friend's mother is worried. - _______________________________________

5. They are very embarrassed. - _______________________________

6. He writes a letter to his mother every week.

    - _______________________________

7. I don't understand. - _______________________________

Exercise WR 3.7

Match each word on the right with the phrase on the left that best fits it:

Verb:	Phrase:
1. Comprar	a. Ropa (Clothes)
2. Vender	b. Café (Coffee)
3. Beber	c. Un libro (Book)
4. Abrir	d. A un amigo (To a friend)
5. Ayudar	e. La puerta (The door)
6. Hablar	f. Un regalo (A gift)
7. Escribir	g. Una carta (A letter)
8. Leer	h. Con sus padres (With their parents)

Exercise WR 3.8

Now, translate the phrases you made in the previous activity:

1. *Comprar un regalo* - _______________________
2. *Vender ropa* - _______________________
3. *Beber café* - _______________________
4. *Abrir la puerta* - _______________________
5. *Ayudar a un amigo* - _______________________
6. *Hablar con sus padres* - _______________________
7. *Escribir una carta* - _______________________
8. *Leer un libro* - _______________________

ANSWERS:

Exercise WR 3.1

1. D (Está en el supermercado.) / 2. A (Trabaja al lado del hospital.) /
3. C (Comer juntos)

Transcript:

Juan: Hola, María. ¿Dónde estás? (Hello, María. Where are you?)

María: Estoy en el supermercado. (I am at the grocery store.)

Juan: ¿Dónde está el supermercado? (Where is the grocery store?)

María: Está al lado del hospital. ¿Qué haces tú? (It's next to the hospital. What are you doing?)

Juan: Estoy en trabajo. Trabajo al lado del hospital. (I am at work. I work next to the hospital.)

María: ¡Qué bien! Estamos cerca. ¿Comemos juntos? (Great! We are close. [Should] we eat together?)

Juan: Sí. Comemos juntos. Hay un restaurante muy cerca. (Yes. [Let's] eat together. There is a restaurant nearby.)

María: Muy bien. (Very good.)

Exercise WR 3.2

1. Los padres de María viven en la ciudad al lado de su tienda. (María's parents live in the city, next to their store.)
2. Sí, venden mucha ropa. (Yes, they sell a lot of clothes.)
3. María asiste a la universidad con su prima Lucía. (María attends university with her cousin Lucía.)
4. La madre de Lucía es cocinera. Cocina muy bien. (Lucía's mother is a chef. She cooks very well.)
5. Sus abuelos viven cerca. (Her grandparents live close.)

Transcript:

Mis padres viven en la ciudad. Viven al lado de su tienda. Tienen una tienda de ropa. Venden mucha ropa. Yo asisto a la universidad con mi prima Lucia. Somos estudiantes. La madre de Lucía es mi tía. Ella trabaja en un restaurante. Ella cocina muy bien. Mis abuelos viven cerca.

(My parents live in the city. They live next to their store. They have a clothes store. They sell a lot of clothes. I attend university with my cousin Lucía. We are students. Lucía's mother is my aunt. She works in a restaurant. She cooks very well. My grandparents live close.)

Exercise WR 3.3

Sample Answer:

Yo vivo en Chicago. Mis hermanos viven en Chicago, también. Mis padres no viven en Chicago. Ellos viven en California. Mi madre es enfermera y mi padre es oficinista. Mi hermano tiene cuatro hijos. Ellos son jóvenes. Mi hermana tiene tres hijos--dos hijas y un hijo. Mi sobrino Mike es alto y divertido. Mis sobrinas son lindas.

(I live in Chicago. My siblings live in Chicago, too. My parents don't live in Chicago. They live in California. My mother is a nurse and my father is an office worker. My brother has four children. They are young. My sister has three children – two daughters and one son. My nephew Mike is tall and funny. My nieces are pretty.)

Exercise WR 3.4

Sample answers:

1. Cuando estoy con mi familia, estoy feliz y tranquila. (When I am with my family, I am happy and calm.)
2. Cuando estoy trabajando, estoy ocupada y agobiada. (When I am working, I am busy and overwhelmed.)
3. Cuando estoy con mis amigos estoy de buen humor y emocionada. (When I am with my friends I am in a good mood and excited.)
4. Cuando estoy de vacaciones estoy relajada. (When I am on vacation I am relaxed.)
5. Cuando tengo que madrugar, estoy enfadada y cansada. (When I have to get up early, I am angry and tired.)

Exercise WR 3.5

Buscar (To look for)

Yo busco (I look for)	Nosotros/as buscamos (We look for)
Tú buscas (You look for)	Vosotros/as buscan (You work)
Él/ Ella/ Usted busca (He/She looks for / You look for)	Ellos/as/ Ustedes buscan (They/ You look for)

Romper (To break)

Yo rompo (I break)	Nosotros/as rompemos (We break)
Tú rompes (You break)	Vosotros/as rompen (You break)
Él/ Ella/ Usted rompe (He/She breaks / You break)	Ellos/as/ Ustedes rompen (They/ You break)

Abrir (To open)

Yo abro (I open)	Nosotros/as abrimos (We open)
Tú abres (You open)	Vosotros abren (You open)
Él/ Ella/ Usted abre (He/She opens / You open)	Ellos/as/ Ustedes abren (They/You open)

Exercise WR 3.6

1. Estamos despistados hoy.
2. ¿Qué cocina?/ ¿Qué está cocinando?
3. ¿Por qué estudias español?
4. La madre de mi amigo está preocupada.
5. Ellos están avergonzados.
6. Él escribe una carta a su madre cada semana.
7. No entiendo/ Yo no comprendo.

Exercise WR 3.7

1. Comprar (F) un regalo
2. Vender (A) ropa
3. Beber (B) café
4. Abrir (E) la puerta
5. Ayudar (D) a un amigo
6. Hablar (H) con sus padres
7. Escribir (G) una carta
8. Leer (C) un libro

Exercise WR 3.8

1. To buy a gift
2. To sell clothes
3. To drink coffee
4. To open the door
5. To help a friend
6. To talk with his/her/your (formal) parents
7. To write a letter
8. To read a book

Week 4, Day 1: The -*Go* Verbs

What's in store for you today: -*go* verbs

Today's goals are:

- To learn about the "-*go*" verbs
- To learn about negations

Listen to Track 4.1.1

Man: *Hola, Carla. ¿Qué haces aquí en el parque?* (Hello, Carla. What are you doing here in the park?)

Woman: *Hola, David. Hago la tarea. ¿Qué haces tú?* (Hello, David. I am doing homework. What are you doing?)

Man: *Yo salgo a correr.* (I am going for a run.)

Woman: *Muy bien. Mi médico dice que es muy buen ejercicio salir a correr.* (Very good. My doctor says it's very good exercise to go running.)

Man: *Yo digo lo mismo. Por eso, salgo a correr tres días de la semana.* (I say the same. Because of this, I go for a run three days a week.)

The -*go* Verbs

What in the world are the -*go* verbs? They aren't verbs that deal with "going" somewhere, if that's what you're thinking. The "-*go*" verbs get their name because of the way they conjugate.

If you remember before, we discussed how *ser, estar,* and *tener* aren't regular verbs. Well, our "-*go*" verbs are going to be irregular as well.

Listen to Track 4.1.2

The important thing to remember about "-*go*" verbs is their name – the change will come in the 1st person singular. So, while **hablar** changes to **yo hablo**, "-*go*" verbs such as **decir** (to say/tell) will change to **yo digo**.

Hacer (To do/To make), and other verbs like it, will be our "-*go*" verbs. Let's take a look at how they conjugate, shall we?

-*Go* Verbs: Group 1

Listen to Track 4.1.3

This first group of verbs will <u>only</u> be irregular in the 1st person singular (*yo*) form. They are:

- *Hacer* – To do/To make
- *Poner* – To put/To place
- *Salir* – To go out/To leave

Listen to Track 4.1.4

Hacer (Do)

Yo hago (I do)	**Nosotros/as hacemos** (We do)
Tú haces (You do)	**Vosotros/as hacéis** (You do)
Él/Ella/Usted hace (He / She does / You do)	**Ellos/as/Ustedes hacen** (They do)

Listen to Track 4.1.5

Poner (Put)

Yo pongo (I put)	**Nosotros/as ponemos** (We put)
Tú pones (You put)	**Vosotros/as ponéis** (We put)
Él/Ella/Usted pone (He / she puts / you put)	**Ellos/as/Ustedes ponen** (They put)

Listen to Track 4.1.6

Salir (Go out)

Yo salgo (I go out)	**Nosotros/as salimos** (We go out)
Tú sales (You go out)	**Vosotros/as salís** (You go out)
Él/Ella/Usted sale (He / She / You go out)	**Ellos/as/Ustedes salen** (They go out)

Exercise 4.1.1

Listen to Track 4.1.7

Fill in the blanks with the correct verbs as you listen to the recording.

1. *Yo* _________________ *ejercicios todos los días.* (I work out every day.)
2. *Lucia y Hector* _________________ *a los bares todos los sábados.* (Lucía and Hector go out to bars every Saturday.)
3. *Nosotros* _________________ *la tarea en casa.* (We do homework at home.)
4. *Yo* _________________ *la comida en la mesa.* (I [will] put the food on the table.)
5. *Ellos* _________________ *de casa a las 8:00.* (They leave their house at 8:00.)

-*Go* Verbs: Group Two

Listen to Track 4.1.8

This next group of verbs will only be irregular in the 1st person singular (*yo*), but you'll notice that the change is a little more than just adding a "-*g*." For this group, we'll look at the verbs:

- *Caer* – To fall
- *Traer* – To bring

Listen to Track 4.1.9

Caer (Fall)

Yo caigo (I fall)	**Nosotros/as caemos** (We fall)
Tú caes (You fall)	**Vosotros/as caéis** (You fall)
Él/Ella/Usted cae (He / she falls / you fall)	**Ellos/as/Ustedes caen** (They fall)

Listen to Track 4.1.10

Traer (Bring)

Yo traigo (I bring)	**Nosotros/as traemos** (We bring)
Tú traes (You bring)	**Vosotros/as traéis** (You bring)
Él/Ella/Usted trae (He / she brings/ you bring)	**Ellos/as/Ustedes traen** (They bring)

Exercise 4.1.2

Conjugate the verbs to match the subjects:

Example:

Answer: Tú **caes**

Caer	*Traer*
Tú	*Ella*
Él	*Ellos*
Nosotras	*Tú*
Ustedes	*Nosotros*
Yo	*Yo*
Vosotros	*Vosotros*

-*Go* Verbs: Group 3

Listen to Track 4.1.11

This next set of -*go* verbs will be a little trickier. There are a lot of changes taking place, so you're really going to want to pay close attention. The verbs we'll look at now are:

- **Decir** – To say/To tell
- **Oír** – To hear

Listen to Track 4.1.12

Decir (Say)

Yo digo (I say)	**Nosotros/as decimos** (We say)
Tú dices (You say)	**Vosotros/as decís** (You say)
Él/Ella/Usted dice (He / she says / you say)	**Ellos/as/Ustedes dicen** (They say)

***Note:** This verb is not only a -*go* verb, it is also a "boot-shoe" or "stem-changing" verb. We will go into that in more detail in the next lesson. For now, pay attention to how in the 1st and 2nd person plural, the stem-change (the vowel change from "e" to "i") doesn't carry over.

Listen to Track 4.1.13

Oír (Hear)

Yo oigo (I hear)	**Nosotros/as oímos** (We hear)
Tú oyes (You hear)	**Vosotros/as oís** (You hear)
Él/Ella/Usted oye (He / she hears/ you hear)	**Ellos/as/Ustedes oyen** (They hear)

Exercise 4.1.3

Listen to Track 4.1.14

Listen to the track and fill in the blanks:

- *No __________ muy bien.* (I don`t __________ very well.)
- *Tú siempre __________ la verdad.* (You always __________ the truth.)
- *¿__________ música? Nosotros __________ música.* (Do you __________ music? We __________ music.)
- *Mis amigos _____ que salimos esta noche.* (My friends _____ that we go out tonight.)
- *Mi hermano _______ que necesitamos leche.* (My brother _____ that we need milk.)

Affirmation and Negation:

Listen to Track 4.1.15

When we want to negate something, we usually say "*no.*" **No tengo cebollas. No trabajo por las mañanas. No viajamos con mucha frecuencia.**

But we can also negate using "negation words." Here, you'll find a list of the most common negation words with their affirmation counterparts:

Nadie – Nobody/No one	**Alguien** – Somebody/Someone
Nada – Nothing	**Algo** – Something
Nunca – Never	**Siempre** – Always
Tampoco – Neither	**También** – Also/Too

Some of these should be familiar to you.

Using Negations:

Listen to Track 4.1.16

Using negations in Spanish is a little different than in English. We can say:

- *Nadie está en casa.* – No one is at home.
- *No está nadie en casa.* – No one is at home.
- *Nunca recibo cartas.* – I never receive letters.
- *No recibo cartas nunca.* – I never receive letters.
- *Nada está aquí.* – Nothing is here.
- *No está nada aquí.* – Nothing is here.

I'm sure you noticed a lot of negative words in some of those sentences. This is because not only are double negatives acceptable in Spanish, they are very common.

If you put your negation word at the beginning of the sentence, you don't need to add an extra "*no*".

Something to note:

Listen to Track 4.1.17

When you answer a question that requires a "no" response, make sure you say "no" twice!

- *¿Siempre llegas tarde a tu trabajo?* (Do you always arrive late to work?)
- *No, no llego tarde a mi trabajo nunca.* (No, I never arrive late to work.) OR
- *No, nunca llego tarde a mi trabajo.* (No, I never arrive late to work.)

A "yes" answer would look like this:

- *Si, siempre llego tarde a mi trabajo.* (Yes, I always arrive late to work.)

Exercise 4.1.4

Match these words with their English equivalents:

1.	*Nadie*	a.	Neither
2.	*Nunca*	b.	Always
3.	*Alguien*	c.	Something
4.	*Algo*	d.	Somebody/Someone
5.	*También*	e.	Nobody/No one
6.	*Nada*	f.	Nothing
7.	*Tampoco*	g.	Also/Too
8.	*Siempre*	h.	Never

Practice Corner

Listening:

Listen to Track 4.1.18

Exercise 4.1.5

Listen to the track and put the sentences in order:

- *pan---el---nunca---nevera---no---pongo---la---en -* _______________________
- *siempre---su---perro---casa---mi---mi---amiga---trae---a -* _______________
- *nada---no---oímos---nosotros -* ___________________________________
- *por---escaleras---las---yo---caigo---siempre -* _______________________
- *dice---el---médico---necesito---que---ejercicio---hacer -* _________________

Writing:

Exercise 4.1.6

Write some sentences about 1) things you never do, 2) things you always do, 3) things your friends and family never do, and 4) things your family and friends always do.

Write as many as you can! Include some of the verbs we learned today, as well as some of the verbs we learned last week.

____

____

____

____

____

Grammar:

Exercise 4.1.7

Conjugate the following verbs:

Example:

Yo _____ (decir)

Answer: Yo <u>digo</u>

Decir

Traer

Hacer

Vocabulary:

Exercise 4.1.8

Answer the following questions:

- *¿Pones la mantequilla (butter) en la nevera?* (Do you put the butter in the refrigerator?)

- *¿Con qué frecuencias caes por las escaleras?* (How often do you fall down the stairs?)

  ____

- *¿Sales con tus amigos los fines de semana* (on weekends)*? (Do you go out with your* friends on weekends?)

  ____

- *¿Siempre dices la verdad?* (Do you always tell the truth?)

  ____

- *¿Oyes algo ahora mismo?* (Do you hear something right now?)

  ____

Additional Vocabulary:

Listen to Track 4.1.19

- **_Tarea_** – Homework
- **_Lo mismo_** – The same
- **_Semana_** – Week
- **_Mantequilla_** – Butter
- **_Escaleras_** – Stairs
- **_Hacer ejercicio_** – To work out

A Quick Recap of this Lesson

Today, we talked about the *-go* verbs.

- They take a "g" in the 1st person singular conjugation.

We also talked about negation.

• **Nadie** – Nobody/no one • **Nada** – Nothing • **Nunca** – Never • **Tampoco** – Neither	• **Alguien** – Somebody/Someone • **Algo** – Something • **Siempre** – Always • **También** – Also/Too

We learned that in Spanish, not only is it okay, but it's very common to use double negatives.

ANSWERS:

Exercise 4.1.1

1. Hago (I do) / 2. Salen (They leave) / 3. Hacemos (We do) / 4. Pongo (I put) / 5. Salen (They leave)

Exercise 4.1.2

Caer: Caes, Cae, Caemos, Caen, Caigo, Caéis
Traer: Trae, Traen, Traes, Traemos, Traigo, Traéis

Exercise 4.1.3

- No oigo muy bien. (I don't hear very well.)
- Tú siempre dices la verdad. (You always tell the truth.)
- ¿Oyes música? Nosotros oímos música. (Do you hear music? We listen to music.)
- Mis amigos dicen que salimos esta noche. (My friends say we go out tonight.)
- Mi hermano dice que necesitamos leche. (My brother says we need milk.)

Exercise 4.1.4

1. E (Nobody/No one)
2. H (Never)
3. D (Somebody/Someone)
4. C (Something)
5. G (Also/Too)
6. F (Nothing)
7. A (Neither)
8. B (Always)

Exercise 4.1.5

- No pongo el pan en la nevera nunca. (I never put the bread in the refrigerator.)
- Mi amiga siempre trae su perro a mi casa. (My friend always brings her dog to my house.)
- Nosotros no oímos nada. (We don't hear anything.)
- Yo siempre caigo por las escaleras. (I always fall down the stairs.)
- El médico dice que necesito hacer ejercicio. (The doctor says I need to work out.)

Exercise 4.1.6

Sample sentences:

Yo siempre hago la cama.

Yo no salgo nunca.

Mis amigos siempre vienen a mi casa.

Mis padres siempre traen su perro a mi casa.

Exercise 4.1.7

Decir

Yo digo (I say)	Nosotros/as decimos (We say)
Tú dices (You say)	Vosotros/as decís (You say)
Él/ Ella/ Usted dice (He/She says / You say)	Ellos/as/ Ustedes dicen (They/You say)

Traer

Yo traigo (I bring)	Nosotros/as traemos (We bring)
Tú traes (You bring)	Vosotros/as traéis (You bring)
Él/ Ella/ Usted trae (He/She brings / You bring)	Ellos/as/ Ustedes traen (They/You bring)

Hacer

Yo hago (I do)	Nosotros/as hacemos (We do)
Tú haces (You do)	Vosotros/as hacéis (You do)
Él/ Ella/ Usted hace (He/She does / You do)	Ellos/as/ Ustedes hacen (They/You do)

Exercise 4.1.8

Sample answers:

- Sí, pongo la mantequilla en la nevera. (Yes, I put the butter in the fridge.)
- Yo nunca caigo por las escaleras. (I never fall down the stairs.)
- No, no salgo con mis amigos los fines de semana. (No, I don't go out with my friends on the weekends.)
- Sí, siempre digo la verdad. (Yes, I always tell the truth.)
- Sí, oigo algo. Escucho música. (Yes, I hear something. I listen to music.)

Week 4, Day 2: Stem-changing Verbs

What's in store for you today: Stem-changing Verbs

Listen to Track 4.2.1

Boy: *Andrea, ¿qué quieres hacer hoy?* (Andrea, what do you want to do today?)

Girl: *Quiero salir con amigos. ¿Qué quieres hacer tú?* (I want to go out with friends. What do you want to do?)

Boy: *Quiero leer en casa.* (I want to read at home.)

Girl: *Vale. Esta noche yo salgo con amigos y tú lees en casa.* (Okay. Tonight I [will] go out with friends and you [will] read at home.)

Boy: *También, necesito fregar.* (Also, I need to do the dishes.)

Girl: *Yo puedo fregar, si quieres.* (I can do the dishes, if you want.)

Boy. *No te preocupes. Friego yo.* (Don't worry. I [will] do the dishes.)

Stem-changing Verbs

If you remember in the last lesson, when we talked about that very handy verb **"decir,"** we mentioned a group of verbs called "boot-shoe" or "stem-changing" verbs. Well, in today's lesson, we're going to really dive in and see what this group of verbs is all about!

For starters, there are three main groups* of "stem-changers." They are:

- *e:i*
- *o:ue*
- *e:ie*

*There are a few other stem-changers sprinkled throughout the Spanish language. But, for today, we're going to focus on these, because they are the most frequent.

What all those letters up there mean is that when a stem*-changing verb falls into one of those categories, the vowel they contain (an *e* for example) will change when conjugated to specific persons (to *i* for example).

*If you remember, we talked about "verb stems" when we learned the *-ar* verbs.

Let's start with the first group.

E:I Stem-changing Verbs

Listen to Track 4.2.2

We have already talked about the verb **decir** ("to say/to tell"). But there are a lot of other verbs that will fall into the category of e:i stem-changers. Some are very useful verbs, such as **repetir** (to repeat) or **competir** (to compete).

Let's work with the verb **pedir** (to ask for) for now, though.

Listen to Track 4.2.3

Pedir (Ask)

Yo pido (I ask)	**Nosotros/as pedimos** (We ask)
Tú pides (You ask)	**Vosotros/as pedís** (You ask)
Él/Ella/Usted pide (He / she asks / you ask)	**Ellos/as/Ustedes piden** (They ask)

Notice how the verb endings are the same as they would be for any other *-ir* verb.

Just as an example of how important it can be to remember your stem-changers, if you were to say this verb "*pedir*" in the 1st person singular <u>without</u> the stem change, you would actually be saying the noun "fart."

(Pedo = fart).

So you definitely want to make sure you remember when to change those vowels!

Rules to Remember

If you remember, back at the beginning of this chapter, we referred to them as "boot-shoe" verbs as well. This is something that we do simply to make it easier for you to remember which of the persons carries the change. If you look at the chart above, and pay attention to the highlighted portions, you could say that it almost looks like a "boot" or a "shoe." It may seem silly, but thinking of it this way is actually very helpful!

However you choose to remember it, though, what's happening is this:

- The stem-change happens in all persons <u>except</u> the 1st person plural (*Nosotros/as*) and 2nd person (familiar) plural (*Vosotros*).
- This will be true for **<u>all</u>** of your stem-changing verbs.
- *-Ar* verbs will still take *-ar* verb endings; *-er* verbs will still take *-er* verb endings; *-ir* verbs will still take *-ir* verb endings. The only thing that changes with the conjugations of these verbs is the <u>stem</u>.

Listen to Track 4.2.4

So, let's go back to the verb **decir** and look at it again.

Decir (Say)

Yo digo (I say)	**Nosotros/as decimos** (We say)
Tú dices (You say)	**Vosotros/as decís** (You say)
Él/Ella/Usted dice (He / she says/ you say)	**Ellos/as/Ustedes dicen** (They say)

So, as you can see, "*decir*" is not only a *-go* verb, it's also a "boot-shoe" – "stem-changing" – verb.

Other common e:i stem-changing verbs

Listen to Track 4.2.5

Below, you'll find a list of common e:i stem-changing verbs. Make sure you jot these down so you can study them later!

- **Reír** – To laugh
- **Seguir*** – To follow
- **Sonreír** – To smile
- **Servir** – To serve

- ***Repetir*** – To repeat
- ***Competir*** – To compete
- ***Pedir*** – To ask for

> ***Note:** *Seguir* is a little strange in the 1st person singular conjugation for pronunciation reasons. Just so you don't get confused, here's how it conjugates:

Listen to Track 4.2.6

Seguir (Follow)

Yo sigo* (I follow)	**Nosotros/as seguimos** (We follow)
Tú sigues (You follow)	**Vosotros/as seguís** (You follow)
Él/Ella/Usted sigue (He / she follows / you follow)	**Ellos/as/Ustedes siguen** (They follow)

> ***Note:** How the "**u**" dropped. Again, this is for pronunciation reasons.

Exercise 4.2.1

Conjugate the following verbs:

Reír

Repetir

O:UE Stem-changing Verbs

Now that you understand the way stem-changing verbs work, the rest of this lesson will be pretty simple! It's just a matter of remembering which verbs fall into which categories. (It might be a good idea to pull out some flashcards here and start jotting these things down!)

Listen to Track 4.2.7

The o:ue stem-changers work just like the e:i that we just saw. Here, we'll find a whole slew of useful verbs – things like ***dormir*** (to sleep) and ***encontrar*** (to find). And we can't forget one of the most used verbs in almost any language: ***poder*** ("to be able to" or you could even say "to can" – even though that doesn't make sense in English). You need it to be able to say proudly, "***yo puedo hablar español***" (I can speak Spanish).

Let's work with the verb ***poder*** so we can see how this group of verbs looks when conjugated.

Listen to Track 4.2.8

Poder (Power)

Yo puedo (I can)	**Nosotros/as podemos** (We can)
Tú puedes (You can)	**Vosotros/as podéis** (You can)
Él/Ella/Usted puede (He / she can / you can)	**Ellos/as/Ustedes pueden** (They can)

Other common o:ue stem-changing verbs

Listen to Track 4.2.9

Below, you'll find a list of other common o:ue stem-changing verbs. Don't forget to write them down!

- **Contar** – To count
- **Mover** – To move
- **Morir** – To die
- **Volver** – To return
- **Probar** – To try

- **Soñar** – To dream
- **Almorzar*** – To have lunch
- **Dormir** – To sleep
- **Encontrar** – To find
- **Poder** – To be able to

*As was mentioned before, in Spain, ***comer*** means to have lunch. ***Almorzar*** can mean (in some places in Spain) "mid-morning snack."

Exercise 4.2.2

Conjugate the following verbs:

Dormir

Volver

E:IE Stem-changing Verbs

Listen to Track 4.2.10

You've made it to the last set of stem-changing verbs! In this set, you'll find verbs like **cerrar** (to close) and **entender** (to understand). Have you ever heard anyone say, "**no entiendo**"? Well, now you know why! You're also going to find another very common and very useful verb in this group: the verb **querer** (to want).

Listen to Track 4.2.11

Querer (Want)

Yo quiero (I want)	**Nosotros/as queremos** (We want)
Tú quieres (You want)	**Vosotros/as queréis** (You want)
Él/Ella/Usted quiere (He / she wants / you want)	**Ellos/as/Ustedes quieren** (They want)

Notice how just the *-e* took the change. The "u" hung around 1) for pronunciation reasons and 2) because it's not affected at all by the stem-change.

Other common e:ie stem-changing verbs

Listen to Track 4.2.12

Here are some more e:ie stem-changers you're going to want to remember!

- *Mentir* – To lie
- *Pensar* – To think
- *Cerrar* – To close
- *Entender* – To understand
- *Encender* – To turn on

- *Fregar** – To wash/To scrub
- *Comenzar* – To begin
- *Perder* – To lose
- *Querer* – To want

* *Fregar* can mean both "to do the dishes" or simply just "to mop", "to scrub" or "to wash."

Exercise 4.2.3

Conjugate the following verbs:

Pensar

Encender

E:IE Bonus Words

Listen to Track 4.2.13

There are two more verbs we're going to look at today: *tener* (to have) and *venir* (to come).

I'm sure you're wondering why they're in their own little category. The answer is simple! They are different than other e:ie stem-changers because they are also *-go* verbs.

Take a look:

Listen to Track 4.2.14

Tener (To have)

Tengo (I have)	**Tenemos** (We have)
Tienes (You have)	**Tenéis** (You have)
Tiene (He / She has / You have)	**Tienen** (They Have)

Exercise 4.2.4

Conjugate the verb *venir*. Remember, it's an e:ie *-go* verb. It's also an *-ir* verb. Lots to keep in mind!

Venir

An Important Grammar Note:

Now that you've learned a whole slew of new verbs, you can make a whole slew of new sentences. And those sentences you make may have more than one verb in them. If this happens, and you're refering to the <u>same</u> subject, your first verb will be conjugated while the second remains in the infinitive form.

Listen to Track 4.2.15

- *Quiero leer el libro.* (I want to read the book.)
- *Mi amigo puede nadar muy bien.* (My friend can swim really well.)
- *Mis amigos y yo queremos salir.* (My friends and I want to go out.)
- *Ellos necesitan visitar a sus padres.* (They need to visit their parents.)

Practice Corner

Listening:

Listen to Track 4.2.16

Exercise 4.2.5

Listen to the conversation and answer the questions (answer in complete sentences!):

1. *¿Qué hace María?* (What is María doing?)

    ____

2. *¿Qué quiere hacer Juan?* (What does Juan want to do?)

    ____

3. *¿Qué sirve el restaurante?* (What does the restaurant serve?)

    ____

Writing:

Exercise 4.2.6

Write out sentences following these prompts:

- *Yo quiero... -* ____
- *Yo puedo... -* ____
- *Mi amigo/padre/novio/etc. quiere -* ____
- *Mi amigo/padre/novio/etc. puede -* ____
- *Mi casa tiene... -* ____
- *Mi padre/ mi madre/ mi amigo tiene... -* ____

Grammar:

Exercise 4.2.7

Conjugate the following verbs:

Servir

Mover

Mentir

Tener

Vocabulary:

Exercise 4.2.8

Translate the following sentences from English into Spanish:

1. I always order chicken and broccoli. - _______________________________
2. My brother never tells the truth. - _______________________________
3. The doctor wants to talk with my friend. - _______________________________
4. I have five siblings. - _______________________________
5. Sometimes, I have lunch in a restaurant. - _______________________________
6. I never sleep on the couch. - _______________________________

A Quick Recap of this Lesson

Today, we talked about stem-changing verbs.

We looked at three main groups:

- E:I
- O:UE
- E:IE

ANSWERS:

Exercise 4.2.1

Reír

Río	Reímos
Ríes	Reís
Ríe	Ríen

Repetir

Repito	Repetimos
Repites	Repetís
Repite	Repiten

Exercise 4.2.2

Dormir

Duermo	Dormimos
Duermes	Dormís
Duerme	Duermen

Volver

Vuelvo	Volvemos
Vuelves	Volvéis
Vuelve	Vuelven

Exercise 4.2.3

Pensar

Pienso	Pensamos
Piensas	Pensáis
Piensa	Piensan

Encender

Enciendo	Encendemos
Enciendes	Encendéis
Enciende	Encienden

Exercise 4.2.4

Vengo	Venimos
Vienes	Venís
Viene	Vienen

Exercise 4.2.5

1. Maria is not doing anything
2. Dinner together with Maria
3. Italian food

Transcript:

Juan: Hola, María. ¿Qué haces? (Hello, María. What are you doing?)

María: No hago nada. Estoy en casa. (I'm not doing anything. I am at home.)

Juan: Ah. ¿Quieres cenar juntos esta noche? (Oh. Do you want to have dinner together tonight?)

María: Sí, puedo cenar contigo. ¿Dónde quieres cenar? (Yes, I can have dinner with you. Where do you want to have dinner?)

Juan: Hay un restaurante nuevo cerca de mi casa. Quiero probar la comida allí. (There is a new restaurant close to my house. I want to try the food there.)

María: ¿Qué sirven? (What do they serve?)

Juan: Sirven comida italiana. (They serve Italian food.)

Exercise 4.2.6

Sample answers:

- Yo quiero comer. (I want to eat.)
- Yo puedo cantar muy bien. (I can sing very well.)
- Mi amigo quiere estudiar francés. (My friend wants to study French.)
- Mi novio quiere salir. (My boyfriend wants to go out.)
- Mi padre puede dibujar muy bien. (My father can draw very well.)
- Mi casa tiene una habitación. (My house has a room.)
- Mi padre tiene pelo rojo. Mi madre tiene pelo largo. Mi amigo tiene ojos azules. (My father has red hair. My mother has long hair. My friend has blue eyes.)

Exercise 4.2.7

Servir

Sirvo	Servimos
Sirves	Servís
Sirve	Sirven

Mover

Muevo	Movemos
Mueves	Movéis
Mueve	Mueven

Mentir

Miento	Mentimos
Mientes	Mentís
Miente	Mienten

Tener

Tengo	Tenemos
Tienes	Tenéis
Tiene	Tienen

Exercise 4.2.8

1. Siempre pido pollo y brócoli.
2. Mi hermano nunca dice la verdad.
3. El médico quiere hablar con mi amigo.
4. Tengo cinco hermanos.
5. A veces, almuerzo en un restaurante.
6. Nunca duermo en el sofá/ No duermo en el sofá nunca

Week 4, Day 3: "*Ir*" and "*Dar*"

What's in store for you today: "Ir" and "Dar" and talking about routines

Listen to Track 4.3.1

Juan: *Hola, María. ¿Qué haces?* (Hello, María. What are you doing?)

María: *Voy a la casa de un amigo.* (I am going to a friend's house.)

Juan: *¿Por qué?* (Why?)

María: *Le doy clases particulares de español.* (I give him private Spanish classes.)

Juan: *¡Qué bien!* (That's good!)

María: *¡Sí! Y tú, ¿adónde vas?* (Yes! And you, where are you going?)

Juan: *Voy a la biblioteca. Necesito estudiar.* (I am going to the library. I need to study.)

María: *¡Buena suerte!* (Good luck!)

Juan: *Gracias.* (Thank you.)

In today's unit, we're going to look at two little verbs - **ir** (to go) and **dar** (to give). Don't let their size fool you, though. They may be small but they are both very big when it comes to how useful and common they are!

They are both irregular verbs, so get ready to write them down! You're going to want to remember these ones, because you'll be using them a lot.

Dar – to give

Listen to Track 4.3.2

Here is how **dar** (give)will conjugate:

Doy (I give)	**Damos** (We give)
Das (You give)	**Dais** (You give)
Da (He / She gives / You give)	**Dan** (They give)

So, that one isn't too bad, right? The only thing really strange about the conjugation is in the 1st person singular: *doy*.

Exercise 4.3.1

Let's check our memory! Conjugate the verb **dar** on your own. See if you can do it without looking back.

Dar

Conjugating *dar* isn't too overly complicated. The next verb we're going to look at, though, is a little more interesting.

Ir- to go

Listen to Track 4.3.3

Here is how you will conjugate **ir** (to go):

Voy (I go)	**Vamos** (Let's go)
Vas (You go)	**Vais** (You go)
Va (He/ She goes)	**Van** (They Go)

Well, that was strange, wasn't it? Not only does **ir** not have a "v" in it, but it looks as if it's conjugating with "**a**"s instead of "**e**"s or "**i**"s like we would expect.

This is probably one of the strangest – yet one of the most commonly used – verbs in any language. So make sure you take some time to study these conjugations!

Exercise 4.3.2

Listen to Track 4.3.4

Listen as the speakers say where they are going, and answer the question: *¿Adónde* van?* (Where are they going/Where do they go?)

Example:

Lucía

Answer: ***Lucía va a la casa de su amigo***. (Lucía is going to her friend's house.)

- *Roberto y sus amigos* (Roberto and his friends) _______________________
- *Los hermanos de José* (Joseph's brothers) _______________________
- *El hijo de Gloria* (Gloria's son) _______________________________

> ***Note:** *"Adónde"* (a+dónde) is asking "to where." We will use it with this verb ***ir***.

Vocabulary:

Today, we're going to start learning how to talk about things we do every day! In order to do that, we need to learn some new vocabulary, though!

Vocabulary: Days of the Week

Listen to Track 4.3.5

- ***El domingo*** – Sunday
- ***El lunes*** – Monday
- ***El martes*** – Tuesday
- ***El miércoles*** – Wednesday
- ***El jueves*** – Thursday
- ***El viernes*** – Friday
- ***El sábado*** – Saturday

> ***Note:** Days of the week **are not** capitalized in Spanish.

Exercise 4.3.3

Match the days in Spanish with their English equivalents:

1.	*martes*	a.	Sunday
2.	*jueves*	b.	Tuesday
3.	*viernes*	c.	Monday
4.	*domingo*	d.	Saturday
5.	*sábado*	e.	Thursday
6.	*lunes*	f.	Wednesday
7.	*miércoles*	g.	Friday

Vocabulary: Hobbies

Listen to Track 4.3.6

Now that we know how to say the days of the week, let's talk about things that we do during the week!

- **Jugar (u:ue)* al...** (To play... [a sport])
  - **Baloncesto** (Basketball)
  - **Béisbol** (Baseball)
  - **Golf** (Golf)
  - **Fútbol** (Soccer)
  - **Fútbol americano** (Football [American football])
  - **Tenis** (Tennis)

- **Tocar...** (To play... [an instrument])
  - **El piano** (The piano)
  - **La guitarra** (The guitar)
  - **El violín** (The violin)
  - **La flauta** (The flute)
  - **La trompeta** (The trumpet)

- **Hacer...** (To do...)
  - **Ejercicio** (Exercise [To work out])
  - **La jardinería** (Gardening)

- o **La lucha** (Wrestling)
- o **El ciclismo** (Cycling)

- **Ir de...** (To go...)
  - o **Caza** (Hunting)
  - o **Pesca** (Fishing)

*You can see that "jugar" is a stem-changing verb by the letters in the parentheses. These vowels let you know what the change is. It will function just like all the other stem-changing "boot-shoe" verbs we've seen: ***Yo juego, Tú juegas, Él juega, Nosotros jugamos, Vosotros jugáis, Ellos juegan***. (I play, You play, He plays, We play, You play, They play.)

Exercise 4.3.4

Listen to Track 4.3.7

Listen to the track and fill in the blanks:

- *El lunes, ___________ al baloncesto.* (On Monday, ___________ basketball.)
- *El domingo, __________ de __________.* (On Sunday, __________ fishing.)
- *Los martes, _____________.* (On Tuesdays, _____________.)
- *Los jueves, _____________.* (On Thursdays, __________.)
- *El sábado, __________ _____________.* (Saturday, __________.)

Something to note:

Listen to Track 4.3.8

When we're talking about something we do "every Monday" or "every Saturday" we use the plural definite article "***los***."

- ***Los lunes trabajo.*** (I work on Mondays.)
- ***Los sábados juego al golf.*** (I play golf on Saturdays.)

If it's something we're only going to do "on Monday" or "on Saturday" we will use the singular definite article.

- ***El lunes voy al médico.*** (On Monday I go to the doctor.)
- ***El sábado toco el piano en concierto.*** (On Saturday I play the piano in concert.)

Practice Corner

Listening:

Listen to Track 4.3.9

Exercise 4.3.5

Listen to the track and fill in the chart:

María tiene una semana muy ocupada. ¿Qué hace esta semana? (María has a very busy week. What is she doing this week?)

El lunes (Mon)	El martes (Tue)	El miércoles (Wed)	El jueves (Thu)	El viernes (Fri)	El sábado (Sat)	El domingo (Sun)

Writing:

Exercise 4.3.6

Pretend this is your schedule for this week. What do you have to do?

	Lunes	Martes	Miércoles	Jueves	Viernes
Por la mañana	Trabajar	Trabajar	Trabajar	Trabajar	Ir de pesca
Por la tarde	Jugar al baloncesto	Ir al médico		Hacer ciclismo	
Por la noche		Cenar con un amigo	Tocar el piano		

Vocabulary:

Exercise 4.3.7

Translate the following sentences from English into Spanish:

1. On Mondays, I go to the store. - ______________________________
2. On Thursday, he is going to his cousin's house. - ______________________
3. On Sunday, I play soccer. - ______________________________
4. On Saturdays, they play soccer. - ______________________________
5. On Wednesday, I am going to the doctor. - ______________________
6. On Tuesday, I wrestle. - ______________________________

Grammar:

Exercise 4.3.8

Fill in the blanks with the correct form of *dar*:

- *Yo te* __________ *la respuesta.* (I give you the answer.)
- *¿Tú me* ________ *la leche?* (Will you give me the milk?)
- *Nosotros* ________ *mucho dinero a las caridades.* (We give a lot of money to charities.)
- *Ellos le* ________ *un portátil nuevo.* (They give her/him a new laptop.)
- *Ella* ________ *clases particulares de Español.* (She gives private Spanish classes.)

Additional Vocabulary:

Listen to Track 4.3.10

Here are some other hobbies you might want to know:

- **Los pasatiempos** (Hobbies)
- **Tocar...** (To play... [a musical instrument])
  - **La guitarra eléctrica** (The electric guitar)
  - **El bajo eléctrico** (The bass guitar)

- o **La batería** (The drumkit)
- o **El saxofón** (The saxophone)
- o **El teclado** (The keyboard)
- o **El clarinete** (The clarinet)

- **Coleccionar** (To collect)
  - o **Sellos** (Stamps)
  - o **Postales** (Postcards)

- **Bailar** (To dance)
  - o **Salsa** (Salsa)
  - o **Merengue** (Merengue)
  - o **Vals** (Waltz)
  - o **Tango** (Tango)

- **Jugar** (To play… [a sport/game])
  - o **A los videojuegos** (Video games)
  - o **A las cartas** (Cards)

- **Patinar sobre hielo** (To ice skate)

- **Patinar sobre línea** (To rollerblade)

- **Patinar sobre ruedas** (To roller skate)

- **Montar a caballo** (To go horseback riding)

- **Sacar fotos** (To take pictures)

A Quick Recap of this Lesson

Today, we looked at the verbs *ir* (to go) and *dar* (to give), which are both irregular.

We also talked about the days of the week:

- **El domingo** – Sunday
- **El lunes** – Monday
- **El martes** – Tuesday
- **El miércoles** – Wednesday
- **El jueves** – Thursday
- **El viernes** – Friday
- **El sábado** – Saturday

And, finally, we discussed hobbies and talked about our daily routines.

ANSWERS:

Exercise 4.3.1

Dar

Yo doy (I give)	Nosotros/as damos (We give)
Tú das (You give)	Vosotros/as dan (You give)
Él/ Ella/ Usted da (He/She gives / You give)	Ellos/as/ Ustedes dan (They/You give)

Exercise 4.3.2

- Lucía va a la casa de su amigo. (Lucía is going to her friend's house.)
- Roberto y sus amigos van a un restaurante nuevo. (Roberto and his friends are going to a new restaurant.)
- Los hermanos de José van a la tienda. (José's brothers are going to the store.)
- El hijo de Gloria va a la Universidad de Florida. (Gloria's son goes to the University of Florida.)

Transcript:

- Hola, soy Lucía. Yo voy a la casa de mi amigo. (Hello, I'm Lucía. I'm going to my friend's house.)

- Buenos días. Me llamo Roberto. Mis amigos y yo vamos a un restaurante nuevo. (Good morning/good day. My name is Roberto. My friends and I are going to a new restaurant.)
- Mi nombre es José. Mis hermanos van a la tienda. (My name is José. My brothers are going to the store.)
- Hola, soy Gloria. Mi hijo va a la Universidad de Florida. (Hello, I'm Gloria. My son goes to the University of Florida.)

Exercise 4.3.3

1. B (Tuesday), 2. E (Thursday), 3. G (Friday), 4. A (Sunday), 5. D (Saturday), 6. C (Monday), 7. F (Wednesday)

Exercise 4.3.4

- El lunes, juego al baloncesto. (On Monday, I play basketball.)
- El domingo, voy de pesca. (On Sunday, I go fishing.)
- Los martes, hago ejercicio. (On Tuesdays, I work out.)
- Los jueves, toco el piano. (On Thursdays, I play piano.)
- El sábado, hago lucha. (On Saturday, I wrestle.)

Exercise 4.3.5

El lunes	El martes	El miércoles	El jueves	El viernes	El sábado	El domingo
Va al dentista y hace ejercicio (Go to the dentist and exercise)	Hace ciclismo y juega al tenis con una amiga (Cycle and play tennis with a friend)	Cena con sus padres (Dinner with his parents)	Hace la lucha y toca la flauta (He fights and plays the flute)	Hace ejercicio y almuerza con su hermana (He exercises and has lunch with his sister)	Hace la jardinería y juega al baloncesto con unos amigos (Gardening and playing basketball with friends)	Va de pesca con su padre (Goes fishing with his father)

Transcript:

Tengo una semana muy ocupada. El lunes, voy al dentista y hago ejercicio. El martes, hago ciclismo y juego al tenis con una amiga. El miércoles, ceno con mis padres. El jueves, hago lucha y toco la flauta. El viernes, hago ejercicio y almuerzo con mi hermana. El sábado, hago la jardinería y juego al baloncesto con unos amigos. Y, el domingo, voy de pesca con mi padre.

(I have a very busy week. On Monday, I go to the dentist and work out. On Tuesday, I go cycling and play tennis with a friend. On Wednesday, I have dinner with my parents. On Thursday, I wrestle and play the flute. On Friday, I work out and have lunch with my sister. On Saturday, I do the gardening and play basketball with some friends. And on Sunday, I go fishing with my dad.)

Exercise 4.3.6

Example:

El lunes por la mañana trabajo. Por la tarde, juego baloncesto. (On Monday morning, I work. In the afternoon, I play basketball.)

Exercise 4.3.7

1. Los lunes, voy a la tienda.
2. El jueves, él va a la casa de su primo.
3. El domingo, juego al fútbol.
4. Los sábados, ellos juegan al fútbol.
5. El miércoles, voy al médico.
6. El martes, hago lucha.

Exercise 4.3.8

Doy, Das, Damos, Dan, Da

Week 4, Day 4: "Hay que" and "Tener que"

What's in store for you today: *Tener que* and *Hay que*, and expressions with "tener."

Today's goals are:

- To learn the expressions "*tener que*" and "*hay que*"
- To learn expressions with "*tener*"

<u>Listen to Track 4.4.1</u>

Juan: *Hola, María. ¿Cómo estás hoy?* (Hello, María. How are you today?)

María: *Estoy muy ocupada.* (I am very busy.)

Juan: *¿Por qué?* (Why?)

María: *Tengo que hacer muchas cosas. Tengo que ir a la biblioteca para devolver un libro. Necesito ir a la casa de mi abuela, y tengo que hablar con un contable. También, tengo que ir al supermercado para comprar comida.* (I have a lot of things to do. I have to go to the library to return a book. I need to go to my grandma's house, and I have to talk with an accountant. Also, I need to go to the grocery store to buy food.)

Juan: *¿Algo más?* (Anything else?)

María: *Bueno, hay que comer. Así que, en algún momento, tengo que cocinar.* (Well, one must eat. So, at some point, I have to cook.)

Juan: *¿Quiéres comer conmigo? Podemos ir a un restaurante.* (Do you want to eat with me? We can go to a restaurant.)

María: *Sí. Muchas gracias. ¡Así, no tengo que hacer la comida!* (Yes! Thank you very much. That way I won't have to make food!)

Talking about Obligation

We all have obligations – things we have to do. Well, today, we're going to look at how to talk about those things in Spanish.

First things first, you have two options for talking about obligation:

- *Hay que* – You have to
- *Tener que* – Have to

"Hay que…"

Listen to Track 4.4.2

The expression *hay que* is used to talk about general obligations. Think of it like saying "one must." For example: *hay que estudiar mucho* (one must study a lot). We could use it to say things like, *hay que limpiar la cocina* (one must clean the kitchen), or *hay que trabajar mucho* (one must work a lot).

We use this expression when we want to make a general statement. It can also add a little bit of emphasis to your statement.

- *Si quieres aprender español, hay que estudiar cada día* (If you want to learn Spanish, one must study every day).

Rules to remember:

Listen to Track 4.4.3

- When using *hay que*, the verb that follows the expression will always be in the infinitive.
- *Hay que estudiar* (one must study); *hay que leer* (one must read); *hay que pensar* (one must think); *hay que seguir* (one must continue).

"Tener que..."

Listen to Track 4.4.4

The expression ***tener que*** is a more personal form of expressing obligation than its counterpart we just discussed. It means "to have to" and can be conjugated to fit different subjects. ***Yo tengo que estudiar*** (I have to study). ***Nosotros tenemos que salir*** (we have to go out). ***Ellos tiene que comer*** (They have to eat).

Rules to Remember:

Listen to Track 4.4.5

- Like with ***hay que***, ***tener que*** will require an infinitive to come after it.
- Don't forget to conjugate "***tener***" to the subject (I, you, he, etc.).
- ***Tienes que abrir la puerta.*** (You have to open the door). ***Vosotros tenéis que ayudar.*** (You – familiar, plural – have to help.) ***¡Tenemos que ganar!*** (We have to win!)

Exercise 4.4.1

Listen to Track 4.4.6

Listen to the recording and fill in the blanks with the correct verb (either ***hay*** or ***tener*** – be aware, you'll have to conjugate ***tener!***).

- *Para hablar español, __________ que estudiar mucho.*
- *Mañana, __________ que ir de compras.*
- *Mi hermana __________ que llamar a nuestros padres.*
- *__________ que pedir un portátil nuevo.*
- *__________ que ir al supermercado.*
- *Para terminar, __________ que empezar.*

Exercise 4.4.2

Listen to Track 4.4.7

Listen to the track, and fill in the table below based on what the speaker says:

Juan tiene que... (Juan has to ...)	*Juan no tiene que...* (Juan does not have to ...)

Expressions with *tener*

Listen to Track 4.4.8

The verb ***tener*** is very useful, for obvious reasons. But you'll find that in Spanish, it's used in situations in which you wouldn't find it in English. For example, we might say "I am cold." But in Spanish, they'll say ***tengo frío*** (I have cold).

Below, you'll find a list of common expressions using *tener*:

- **Tener calor** (To be hot)
- **Tener frío** (To be cold)
- **Tener hambre** (To be hungry)
- **Tener sed** (To be thirsty)
- **Tener sueño** (To be sleepy)

- **Tener miedo** (To be afraid)
- **Tener prisa** (To be in a hurry)
- **Tener ganas de** (To feel like)
- **Tener X años** (To be X years old)

Exercise 4.4.3

Listen to Track 4.4.9

Listen to the track and fill in the blanks with the correct "*tener*" expression.

1. ___________. *¿Podemos encender el aire acondicionado?* (Can we turn on the air conditioning?)

2. *¿Cuándo comemos?* ________________. (When do we eat? ____________.)

3. *Hacer ejercicio es duro.* ____________ *mucha* ____________. (Exercising is hard. ____________ a lot ____________.)

4. *No quiero trabajar.* ________________. (I don't want to work. ____________.)

5. *Lo siento. No puedo hablar.* ____________. (I'm sorry. I can not talk. ____________.)

6. *Mis amigos* ____________ *salir esta noche.* (My friends ____________ go out tonight.)

7. *Ella* ____________. *¿Podemos encender la calefacción?* (She ____________. Can we turn on the heating?)

8. *Está muy oscuro. ¿*____________*?* (It is very dark. ____________?)

9. *El primo de mi amigo* ____________ *treinta y cuatro* ____________. (My friend's cousin ____________ thirty-four ____________.)

Practice Corner

Listening:

Listen to Track 4.4.10

Exercise 4.4.4

Listen as the speaker makes some statements. Then choose the correct advice to give from the list.

Problema/ Declaración (Problem/Statement)	Consejos (Advice)
1. Tengo frío. 2. Tengo que estudiar. 3. Necesito ir al dentista. Tengo miedo. 4. Tengo hambre. 5. Necesito comida. 6. Siempre tengo sueño. 7. Quiero ganar (earn) más dinero.	a. No hay que tener miedo. Es un hombre simpático. b. Tienes que ir al supermercado. c. Tienes que ponerte (put on) una chaqueta. d. Hay que trabajar más. e. Tienes que dormir más. f. Tienes que comer. g. Tienes que apagar (turn off) la televisión.

Writing:

Exercise 4.4.5

Answer the following questions:

- *¿Cuántos años tienes?* (How old are you?)

  ____

- *¿Qué tienes que hacer hoy?* (What do you have to do today?)

  ____

- *¿Tienes frío ahora mismo?* (Are you cold right now?)

  ____

- *¿Tienes ganas de salir este fin de semana* (this weekend)? (Do you feel like going out this weekend?)

____

Grammar/Vocabulary:

Exercise 4.4.6

Translate the following sentences from Spanish into English:

1. *Hay que comer un desayuno (breakfast) grande.*

   - ___________________________________

2. *Tienes que caminar parallegar a la escuela.*

   - ___________________________________

3. *Tenemos mucho frío. -* ___________________________________

4. *Mis padres tienen ganas de comer comida italiana.*

   - ___________________________________

5. *En este trabajo, hay que ser muy paciente (patient).*

   - ___________________________________

6. *Ellos tienen sueño. -* ___________________________________

7. *Tengo prisa. No quiero llegar tarde al trabajo.*

   - ___________________________________

A Quick Recap of this Lesson

Today, we talked about using **hay que** and **tener que** to express obligation:

- *Hay que* is used with general statements.
- *Tener que* is more personal.
- Both will be followed by an infinitive.

We also talked about expressions using **tener**:

- **Tener calor** (To be hot)
- **Tener frío** (To be cold)
- **Tener hambre** (To be hungry)
- **Tener sed** (To be thirsty)
- **Tener sueño** (To be sleepy)
- **Tener miedo** (To be afraid)
- **Tener prisa** (To be in a hurry)
- **Tener ganas de** (To feel like)
- **Tener X años** (To be X years old)

ANSWERS:

Exercise 4.4.1

Para hablar español, hay que estudiar mucho. (In order to speak Spanish, one must study a lot.)

Mañana, tengo que ir de compras. (Tomorrow, I have to go shopping.)

Mi hermana tiene que llamar a nuestros padres. (My sister has to call our parents.)

Hay que pedir un portátil nuevo. (One must order a new laptop.)

Tenemos que ir al supermercado. (We have to go to the grocery store.)

Para terminar, hay que empezar. (In order to finish, one must start.)

Exercise 4.4.2

Juan tiene que... (Juan has to ...)

- Ir al supermercado (Go to the supermarket)
- Limpiar su casa (Clean his house)
- Visitar a un amigo en el hospital (Visit a friend in the hospital)

Juan no tiene que... (Juan doesn't have to ...)

- Limpiar la cocina (Clean the kitchen)
- Trabajar (Work)
- Cocinar (Cook)

Transcript:

Hoy tengo mucho que hacer. Tengo que ir al supermercado. También, tengo que limpiar mi casa. Pero no tengo que limpiar la cocina. Tengo que visitar a un amigo en el hospital. Pero es sábado y no tengo que trabajar. Tampoco tengo que cocinar. Hoy, ceno con un amigo.

(Today, I have a lot to do. I have to go to the grocery store. Also, I have to clean my house. But I don't have to clean the kitchen. I have to visit a friend in the hospital. But it's Saturday and I don't have to work. I don't have to cook, either. Today, I am having dinner with a friend.)

Exercise 4.4.3

1. Tengo calor (I am hot)
2. Tenemos hambre (We are hungry)
3. Tengosed (I am thirsty)
4. Tengo sueño (I am sleepy)
5. Tengo prisa (I am in a hurry)
6. tienen ganas de (feel like)
7. tiene frío (is cold)
8. Tienes miedo (You are afraid)
9. tiene, años (is, years old)

Transcript:

Tengo calor. ¿Podemos encender el aire acondicionado? (I am hot. Can we turn on the air conditioning?)

¿Cuándo comemos? Tenemos hambre. (When do we eat? We're hungry.)

Hacer ejercicio es duro. Tengo mucha sed. (Working out is hard. I am very thirsty.)

No quiero trabajar. Tengo sueño. (I don't want to work. I'm sleepy.)

Lo siento. No puedo hablar. Tengo prisa. (I'm sorry. I can't talk. I'm in a hurry.)

Mis amigos tienen ganas de salir esta noche. (My friends feel like going out tonight.)

Ella tiene frío. ¿Podemos encender la calefacción? (She is cold. Can we turn on the heating?)

Es muy oscuro. ¿Tienes miedo? (It's very dark. Are you afraid?)

El primo de mi amigo tiene trcinta y cuatro años. (My friend's cousin is thirty-four years old.)

Exercise 4.4.4

1. C   2.G   3.A   4.F   5.B   6.E   7.D

Translations:

Problema/ Declaración (Problem/Statement)	**Consejos** (Advice)
1. I'm cold 2. I have to study. 3. I need to go to the dentist. I'm scared. 4. I'm hungry 5. I need food. 6. I'm always sleepy. 7. I want to earn more money.	a. You don't need to (One mustn't) be scared. He is a nice man. b. You have to go to the grocery store. c. You have to put on a jacket. d. You need to (One must) work more. e. You have to sleep more. f. You have to eat. g. You have to turn off the television.

Exercise 4.4.5

- Tengo 25 años (I am 25 years old)
- Tengo que estudiar. (I have to study)
- No tengo frío. (I am not cold)
- Si tengo ganas de salir este fin de semana. (Yes, I feel like going out this weekend)

Exercise 4.4.6

a. One must eat a big breakfast.

b. You have to walk in order to get to the school.

c. We are very cold.

d. My parents feel like eating Italian (food).

e. In this job, one must be very patient.

f. They are sleepy.

g. I'm in a hurry. I don't want to arrive late to work.

Week 4, Day 5: Telling Time

What's in store for you today: Telling time and Learning Dates

Listen to Track 4.5.1

Hombre: *¿Qué hora es?* (What time is it?)

Mujer: *Son las tres y cuarto. ¿Por qué?* (It's 3:15. Why?)

Hombre: *Tengo que estar en la casa de mi tía a las cuatro y media.* (I have to be at my aunt's house at 4:30.)

Mujer: *¿Está lejos?* (Is it far?)

Hombre: *No. Está al lado del restaurante.* (No. It's next to the restaurant.)

Mujer: *Sí. Está muy cerca.* (Yes. It is very close.)

Hombre: *Tengo que salir de aquí a las cuatro en punto.* (I have to leave here at 4:00 on the dot.)

¿Qué hora es?

If you remember, when we were talking about *ser* and *estar*, we discussed how we will use *ser* when talking about time. As promised, today we're going to learn how to do just that.

Listen to Track 4.5.2

When answering the question, ***¿Qué hora es?*** ("What time is it?"), there are two important expressions to keep in mind:

- ***Son las...***
  - ***Son las dos.*** (It is 2:00.)
  - ***Son las cinco.*** (It is 5:00.)
  - ***Son las diez.*** (It is 10:00.)

- ***Es la...***
  - ***Es la una.*** (It is 1:00.)

- We use "*son las*" with any number that <u>isn't "one."</u>

- We use "*es la*" with "one."

- We use the feminine definite articles ("*la*" and "*las*") because we are referring to the time (***la hora***-The time).

¿Y or Menos? (And Or Less?)

Listen to Track 4.5.3

In English, sometimes we say, "It's a quarter past..." or "It's a quarter to...". Using ***y*** (and) and ***menos*** (minus) in Spanish is kind of like that (only a lot more frequent).

- ***Son las dos y cuarto.*** (It is 2:15 [a quarter past two].)
- ***Son las dos menos cuarto.*** (It is 1:45 [a quarter to two].)

> **Take Note:**   ***Cuarto*** means "quarter."

We don't just use "*y*" and "*menos*" with ***cuarto***, though. We use it all the time!

- ***Son las cinco y veinte.*** (It is 5:20.)
- ***Es la una menos cinco*.*** (It is 12:55.)

> ***Note:** Even though it's "**12:55**" we will say "**one minus five.**" This means that we will need to say "***es la***" since we will be saying "***una.***"
>
> * Another note: We use "*una*" for one because, again, time is feminine.

How to know when to use "*Y*" and when to use "*Menos*"

Listen to Track 4.5.4

Deciding when to use "*y*" (*and*) and when to use "*menos*" (*minus*) is simple:

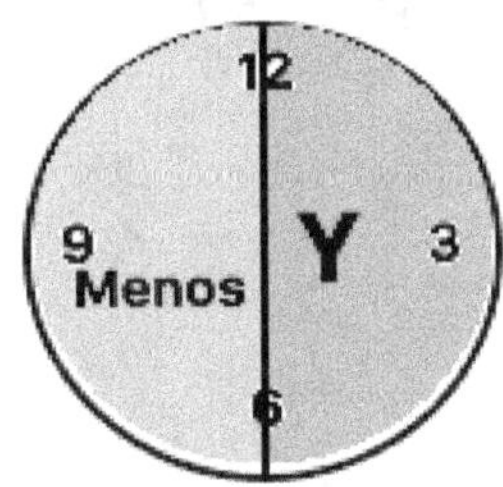

- If it's before :30, use "*y*"
  - Equation: [Hour] y [minutes]
    - It's 12:06. – ***son las doce y seis***
    - It's 1:23. – ***es la una y veintitrés***
    - It's 9:29. – ***son las nueve y veintinueve***

- If it's after :30, use "*menos.*"
  - Equation: [Hour approaching] menos [minutes until that hour]
    - It's 10:47. – ***son las once menos trece*** (eleven minus thirteen).
    - It's 7:41. – ***son las ocho menos diecinueve*** (eight minus nineteen).
    - It's 12:53. – ***es la una menos siete*** (one minus seven).

In theory, telling time in Spanish isn't that difficult. What makes it a little bit of a challenge is changing your way of thinking. Getting used to subtracting the minutes from the hour may take a little time. But if you keep practicing, you'll get used to it. Promise.

Y media

Listen to Track 4.5.5

We've talked about what to do when the minutes fall before or after the halfway mark. Now, let's look at what to do when it's :30 on the dot:

- ***Son las once y media.*** (It's 11:30.)
- ***Es la una y media.*** (It's 1:30.)
- ***Son las tres y media.*** (It's 3:30.)

You will use ***y***, and the word ***media*** (half). You will <u>never</u> say ***menos media***.

Exercise 4.5.1

Answer the question, ***¿Qué hora es?***: (What time is it?):

1. 11:20 - ___________________
2. 7:15 - ___________________
3. 9:45 - ___________________
4. 1:24 - ___________________

5. 2:30 - ___________________
6. 1:55 - ___________________
7. 12:33 - ___________________

¿A qué hora es...? (At what time is it...?)

Listen to Track 4.5.6

To answer the question, "What time is... at?" we will use the following expressions:

- ***A las*** (At)...
  - ***A las diez.*** (At ten.)
  - ***A las seis y media.*** (At half past six.)
  - ***A las ocho menos cinco.*** (At five to eight.)

- ***A la una*** (At one)
  - ***A la una y media.*** (At half past one.)
  - ***A la una y cuarto.*** (At a quarter past one.)
  - ***A la una menos diez.*** (At a quarter past one.)

Things to note:

- *Las* is used with numbers <u>higher than "one."</u>
- *La* is used with "one."

Morning? Noon? Or Night?

We may want to explain that we're talking about 8:00 in the morning, or 12:00 noon. Here are the expressions we need to do that:

Listen to Track 4.5.7

- ***De la mañana*** – In the morning
- ***De la tarde*** – In the afternoon
- ***De la noche*** – At night
- ***El mediodía*** – Noon
- ***La medianoche*** – Midnight

Before, we talked about the expressions ***por la mañana, por la tarde***, and ***por la noche***. Those are used for <u>non-specified times</u>. When we use the preposition ***de*** instead of ***por***, we are talking about a specific time.

For example: ***Tengo una reunión a las ocho de la noche.*** (I have a meeting at 8:00 pm.) VS. ***Tengo una reunión hoy por la noche*** (I have a meeting tonight.).

Here is how we use ***mediodía*** or ***medianoche***:

- ***Es mediodía.*** (It's noon.)
- ***Es medianoche.*** (It's midnight.)
- ***Al mediodía.*** (At noon.)
- ***A la medianoche.*** (At midnight.)

Exercise 4.5.2

Listen to Track 4.5.8

Listen and answer the questions:

1. *¿Qué hora es?* (What time is it?)
   a. 12:15   b. 1:00   c. 12:00   d. 2:00
2. *A qué hora tienes que estar en la reunión?* (What time do you have to be in the meeting?)
   a. 3:45   b. 3:15   c. 4:15   d. 2:45

3. *¿A qué hora tiene que llamar a su jefe?* (What time do you have to call your boss?)

    a. 4:50   b. 5:10   c. 4:10   d. 6:10

4. *¿A qué hora cena con los padres de la mujer?* (What time does he have dinner with the woman's parents?)

    a. 6:00   b. 5:30   c. 7:30   d. 6:30

Vocabulary: *En el trabajo...*

Listen to Track 4.5.9

For our last vocabulary section of this book we're going to look at things that we have all had to do at one point or another. We're going to talk about typical "workplace" activities.

- ***Ir a una reunión*** – To go to a meeting
- ***Dirigir una reunión*** – To chair a meeting
- ***Hacer una llamada*** – To make a call
- ***Hacer fotocopias*** – To make photocopies
- ***Enviar un fax*** – To send a fax
- ***Contestar el teléfono*** – To answer the phone
- ***Responder a correos electrónicos*** – To reply to emails
- ***Llamar a clientes*** – To call clients
- ***Tener una cita con**** – To have an appointment with

*Fun side note: ***Tener una cita*** can also mean "To have a date." ***Esta noche tengo una cita con María.*** (Tonight I have a date with María).

Exercise 4.5.3

Translate the following sentences from Spanish into English.

1. *A las once de la noche, tengo que llamar a un cliente en China.*

    ____

2. *A la una, tengo que hacer una llamada muy importante.*

    ____

3. *A las tres menos cuarto, dirijo* una reunión.*

    ____

4. *A las diez y veinte tengo una cita con un contable.*

   ____

5. *Todo el día tengo que responder a correos electrónicos.*

   ____

*Notice the spelling change. This is for pronunciation purposes, and is only found in the 1st person singular (*yo*) conjugation.

Practice Corner

Listening:

Listen to track 4.5.10

Exercise 4.5.4

Listen as Juan talks about what he has to this week. Fill in his schedule.

	Lunes	Martes	Miércoles	Jueves	Viernes
8:00					
11:15					
12:30					
5:45					
10:00					

Writing:

Exercise 4.5.5

Write out what you have to do today, tomorrow, and the next day. Try to use as many specific times as you can.

____

____

____

____

Grammar:

Exercise 4.5.6

Answer the question, *¿Qué hora es?* (What time is it?)

1. 12:45 am - _____________________
2. 6:12 am - _____________________

3. 8:39 pm - _____________________
4. 2:15 pm - _____________________

5. 1:00 pm - ______________________   7. 12:00 am - ______________________

6. 11:28 pm - ______________________

Vocabulary:

Exercise 4.5.7

Answer these questions. Try to use complete sentences:

- *En tu trabajo, ¿tienes que hacer muchas llamadas?* (In your job, do you have to make a lot of phone calls?)

  ____

- *¿Mañana tienes que ir una reunión?* (Tomorrow, do you have to go to a meeting?)

  ____

- *¿Tienes que responder a muchos correos electrónicos en tu día a día?* (Do you have to reply to a lot of emails day to day?)

  ____

- *¿Envías muchos faxes?* (Do you send a lot of faxes?)

  ____

- *En tu trabajo, ¿qué dices al contestar el teléfono?* (At your job, what do you say upon answering the phone?)

  ____

- *¿Haces muchas fotocopias?* (Do you make a lot of photocopies?)

  ____

Additional Vocabulary:

Listen to Track 4.5.11

Here are a few more words you might want to know:

- **Antes de (+infinitive)** (Before... -ing)
- **Después de (+ infinitive)** (After... -ing)
- **Jefe** (Boss)
- **Gracias por llamar a...** (Thank you for calling...)
- **Día a día** (Day to day)
- **En punto** (On the dot)

A Quick Recap of this Lesson

Today, we talked about telling time:

- We discussed using "*y*" for times before :30.
- And using "*menos*" for times after :30.

We also looked at using:

- *Son las...*
- *Es la...*

and

- *A las...*
- *A la...*

And, finally, we looked at "workplace" vocabulary.

ANSWERS:

Exercise 4.5.1

1. Son las once y veinte
2. Son las siete y cuarto.
3. Son las diez menos cuarto.
4. Es la una y veinticuatro.
5. Son las dos y media.
6. Son las dos menos cinco.
7. Es la una menos veintisiete.

Exercise 4.5.2:

1. C (12:00) / 2. B (3:15) / 3. A (4:50) / 4. D (6:30)

Transcript:

Hombre: ¿Qué hora es? (What time is it?)

Mujer: Es mediodía. (It's noon.)

Hombre: Gracias. (Thank you.)

Mujer: ¿A qué hora tienes que estar en la reunión? (What time do you have to be in the meeting?)

Hombre: A las tres y cuarto. Y después, a las cinco menos diez, tengo que llamar a mi jefe. (At 3:15. And afterwards, at 4:50, I have to call my boss.)

Mujer: Y cenamos con mis padres hoy a las seis y media. (And we are having dinner with my parents today at 6:30.)

Exercise 4.5.3

1. At 11:00 pm, I have to call a client in China.
2. A 1:00 I have to make a very important phone call.
3. At 2:45 I chair a meeting.
4. At 10:20 I have an appointment with an accountant.
5. All day, I have to respond to emails.

Exercise 4.5.4

	Lunes	Martes	Miércoles	Jueves	Viernes
8:00	Trabaja (Works)	Trabaja (Works)	Trabaja (Works)	Tiene que ir al supermercado (Have to go to the supermarket)	
11:15	Tiene que ir a una reunión (Have to go to a meeting)		Tiene que hacer una llamada importante. (Have to make an important call.)	Come con unos amigos en su casa. (Eat with friends at home.)	
12:30	Come con un cliente (Eat with a customer)				Tiene que viajar a Inglaterra. (Have to travel to England.)

5:45		Tiene que ir al médico. (Have to go to the doctor.)		Cena con sus padres. (Dinner with his parents.)	
10:00			Tiene que dormir. (Have to sleep.)		

Transcript:

El lunes, martes, y miércoles, tengo que trabajar a las 8:00. El lunes a las once y cuarto, tengo una reunión. A las doce y media, tengo que comer con un cliente. El martes, a las seis menos cuarto, tengo que ir al médico. El miércoles, a las once y cuarto, tengo que hacer una llamada muy importante. Y a las diez de la noche, tengo que dormir. El jueves no tengo que trabajar. A las ocho de la mañana, tengo que ir al supermercado. A las once y cuarto, como con unos amigos en mi casa. A las seis menos cuarto, ceno con mis padres. El viernes, a las doce y media, tengo que viajar a Inglaterra. Tengo trabajo en Londres.

(On Monday, Tuesday, and Wednesday, I have to work at 8:00. On Monday at 11:15, I have a meeting. At 12:30, I have to eat with a client. On Tuesday, at 5:45, I have to go to the doctor. On Wednesday, at 11:15, I have to make a very important phone call. And at 10:00 pm, I have to sleep. On Thursday, I don't have to work. At 8:00 am, I have to go to the grocery store. At 11:15, I [am] eat[ing] with some friends at my house. At 5:45, I [am] have[ing] dinner with my parents. On Friday, at 12:30, I have to travel to England. I have work in London.)

Exercise 4.5.5

Hoy tengo que ir a trabajar_a las 9:00 am, voy a comer con mis amigos a las 2:00 pm, a las cinco y media tengo que regresar a mi casa. Mañana tengo que ver a mis padres, a las 6:00 pm estudio español y a las 8:00 pm voy al cine. El día despues de mañana voy a estar con clientes todo el día y a las 9:00 pm veo a mi novio en un bar. (Today I have to yo work at 9:00 am , I am going to eat with my friends at 2:00 pm, at half past five I have to go home.Tomorrow I have to see my parents, at 6:00 pm I study spanish and at 8:00 pm I go to the movies. The day after tomorrow I will be with clients all day and at 9:00 pm I see my boyfriend at a bar)

Exercise 4.5.6

1. Es la una menos cuarto.
2. Son las seis y doce.
3. Son las nueve menos veintiuno.
4. Son las dos y cuarto.
5. Es la una.
6. Son las once y veintiocho.
7. Es medianoche.

Exercise 4.5.7

Sample answers:

- Sí. En mi trabajo, hago muchas llamadas. (Yes, in my job, I make a lot of calls.)
- No, mañana no tengo que ir a una reunión. (No, I don't have to go to a meeting tomorrow.)
- No, no respondo a muchos correos electrónicos en mi día a día. (No, I don't respond to a lot of emails day to day.)
- No, no mando faxes nunca. (No, I never send faxes.)
- En mi trabajo, digo "hola" al contestar el teléfono. (At work, I say, "hello" upon answering the phone.)
- No, nunca hago fotocopias. (No, I never make photocopies.)

Week 4 Recap

This week, we talked about irregular verbs. We learned about *-go* verbs, and stem-changers, and we did some more work with the verb *tener*. Let's review what we've learned!

Listening:

Listen to Track WR 4.1

Exercise WR 4.1

Listen to the track and answer the questions (answer with complete sentences):

1. *¿Qué hace Juan?* (What is Juan doing?)

   ____

2. *¿Qué tiene que hacer Juan el sábado?* (What does Juan have to do on Saturday?)

   ____

3. *¿Cuándo es la fiesta para el cumpleaños de la madre de Juan?* (When is the party for Juan's mother's birthday?)

   ____

Listen to Track WR 4.2

Exercise WR 4.2

Listen to the track and fill in the blanks:

Hombre: *¿Qué ___________ hacer hoy?*
Mujer: *Yo ___________ ir a la biblioteca. Busco un libro nuevo para leer.*

Hombre: *Yo tengo que ir a la biblioteca, también. ____________ ir juntos.*
Mujer: *Muy bien. Y después, ___________ ir al parque. ____________ un picnic allí.*

Hombre: *¿____________ traer mi perro?*
Mujer: *¡Por supuesto!*

Hombre: *Pero, _______ _______ ______, tengo que estar en casa. Tengo que llamar a mi jefe. Está en Argentina ahora.*
Mujer: *¿Qué ________ allí?*

Hombre: *Tiene que* ________ ________ ________ *con algunos clientes importantes. Le tengo que llamar porque le necesito* ________ *algunos informes importantes antes de su reunión.*

Writing:

Exercise WR 4.3

Write out your plans for today. Don't forget to include the time!

____

____

____

____

Exercise WR 4.4

Answer these questions with complete sentences.

- *¿Qué tienes que hacer los lunes por la mañana?* (What do you have to do on Monday mornings?)

  ____

- *¿Qué tienes que hacer los martes por la tarde?* (What do you have to do on Tuesday afternoons?)

  ____

- *¿Qué tienes que hacer los miércoles después de comer?* (What do you have to do on Wednesdays after eating [having lunch]?)

  ____

- *¿Tienes que hacer algo los jueves por la tarde?* (Do you have to do anything on Thursday afternoons?)

  ____

- *¿Sales con tus amigos los viernes por la noche?* (Do you go out with your friends on Friday nights?)

  ____

Grammar:

Exercise WR 4.5

Conjugate the following verbs:

Hacer (To do/To make)

Oír (To hear)

Servir (To serve)

Contar (To count)

Perder (To lose)

Tener (To have)

Exercise WR 4.6

Answer the question, *¿Qué hora es?* (What time is it?)

1. 8:15 pm - _______________________
2. 2:58 pm - _______________________
3. 9:23 am - _______________________
4. 11:45 am - _______________________

5. 1:30 pm - _______________________
6. 1:55 am - _______________________
7. 12:00 (noon) - _______________________

Vocabulary:

Exercise WR 4.7

Translate the following sentences from English into Spanish:

1. On Monday, we need to go to the store.

   ____

2. She is hungry. We need to find a restaurant.

   ____

3. They want to read at home this weekend.

   ____

4. My sister does the dishes on Thursdays.

   ____

5. I'm cold. Do you have a blanket?

   ____

6. My nephew is twelve years old.

   ____

7. You never lie. You are very honest.

   ____

8. Her friends give dance classes on Sundays.

   ____

ANSWERS:

Exercise WR 4.1

1. Juan va a la tienda (Juan is going to the store.)
2. Juan tiene que trabajar el sábado. (Juan has to work on Saturday.)
3. La fiesta es el domingo. (The party is on Sunday.)

Transcript:

María: Hola, Juan. ¿Qué haces? (Hello, Juan. What are you doing?)

Juan: Voy a la tienda. (I'm going to the store.)

María: ¿Por qué? (Why?)

Juan: Tengo que comprar un regalo para mi madre. Su cumpleaños es el sábado. (I have to buy a gift for my mother. Her birthday is on Saturday.)

María: ¿El sábado? Pero tienes que trabajar el sábado. (Saturday? But you have to work on Saturday.)

Juan: Sí, pero la fiesta es el domingo. (Yes, but the party is on Sunday.)

Exercise WR 4.2

Hombre: ¿Qué quieres hacer hoy? (What do you want to do today?)

Mujer: Yo quiero ir a la biblioteca. Busco un libro nuevo para leer. (I want to go to the library. I'm looking for a new book to read.)

Hombre: Yo tengo que ir a la biblioteca, también. Podemos ir juntos. (I have to go to the library, too. We can go together.)

Mujer: Muy bien. Y después, podemos ir al parque. Hacemos un picnic allí. (Very good. And afterwards, we can go to the park. We can have a picnic there.)

Hombre: ¿Puedo traer mi perro? (Can I bring my dog?)

Mujer: ¡Por supuesto! (Of course!)

Hombre: Pero, a las cuatro, tengo que estar en casa. Tengo que llamar a mi jefe. Está en Argentina ahora. (But at 4:00 I have to be at home. I have to call my boss. He is in Argentina right now.)

Mujer: ¿Qué hace allí? (What is he doing there?)

Hombre: Tiene que dirigir una reunión con algunos clientes importantes. Le tengo que llamar porque le necesito dar algunos informes importantes antes de su reunión. (He has to chair a meeting with some important clients. I have to call him because I need to give him some important reports before his meeting.)

Exercise WR 4.3

Sample answer:

Hoy, tengo que estudiar español. Estudio español a las siete de la mañana. Después, voy al trabajo. Trabajo a las nueve. A las once y media, como con unos amigos en un restaurante cerca de mi oficina. A las cuatro, salgo del trabajo. A las cinco, ceno. A las seis y cuarto, veo la televisión con mi marido.

(Today, I have to study Spanish. I study Spanish at 7:00 am. Afterwards, I go to work. I work at 9:00. At 11:30, I eat with some friends in a restaurant close to my office. At 4:00, I leave [go out from] work. At 5:00 I have dinner. At 6:15, I watch TV with my husband.)

Exercise WR 4.4

Sample answers:

- Los lunes por la mañana, tengo que trabajar. (On Monday mornings, I have to work.)
- Los martes por la tarde, tengo que limpiar la casa. (On Tuesday afternoons, I have to clean the house.)
- Los miércoles, después de comer, tengo que contestar correos electrónicos. (On Wednesdays after eating, I have to answer emails.)
- No, no tengo que hacer nada los jueves por la tarde. (No, I don't have to do anything on Thursday afternoons.)
- Sí, siempre salgo con mis amigos los viernes por la noche. (Yes, I always go out with my friends on Friday nights.)

Exercise WR 4.5

Hacer (To do/To make)

Yo hago (I do)	Nosotros/as hacemos (We do)
Tú haces (You do)	Vosotros/as hacen (You do)
Él/ Ella/ Usted hace (He/She does / You do)	Ellos/as/ Ustedes hacen (They/You do)

Oír (To hear)

Yo oigo (I hear)	Nosotros/as oimos (We hear)
Tú oyes (You hear)	Vosotros/as oyen (You hear)
Él/ Ella/ Usted oye (He/She hears / You hear)	Ellos/as/ Ustedes oyen (They/You hear)

Servir (To serve)

Yo sirvo (I serve)	Nosotros/as servimos (We serve)
Tú sirves (You serve)	Vosotros/as sirven (You serve)
Él/ Ella/ Usted sirve (He/She serves / You serve)	Ellos/as/ Ustedes sirven (They/You serve)

Contar (To count)

Yo cuento (I count)	Nosotros/as contamos (We count)
Tú cuentas (You count)	Vosotros/as cuentan (You count)
Él/ Ella/ Usted cuenta (He/She counts / You count)	Ellos/as/ Ustedes cuentan (They/You count)

Perder (To lose)

Yo pierdo (I lose)	Nosotros/as perdemos (We lose)
Tú pierdes (You lose)	Vosotros/as pierden (You lose)
Él/ Ella/ Usted pierde (He/She loses / You lose)	Ellos/as/ Ustedes pierden (They/You lose)

Tener (To have)

Yo tengo (I have)	Nosotros/as tenemos (We have)
Tú tienes (You have)	Vosotros/as tienen (You have)
Él/ Ella/ Usted tiene (He/She has / You have)	Ellos/as/ Ustedes tienen (They/You have)

Exercise WR 4.6

1. Son las ocho y cuarto de la noche.
2. Son las tres menos dos de la tarde.
3. Son las nueve y veintitrés de la mañana.
4. Son las doce menos cuarto de la mañana.
5. Es la una y media de la tarde.
6. Son las dos menos cinco de la mañana.
7. Es mediodía.

Exercise WR 4.7

1. El lunes, necesitamos ir a la tienda.
2. Ella tiene hambre. Necesitamos encontrar un restaurante.
3. Ellos quieren leer en casa este fin de semana.
4. Mi hermana friega los platos los jueves.
5. Tengo frío. ¿Tienes una manta?
6. Mi sobrino tiene doce años.
7. Tú nunca mientes/ No mientes nunca.
8. Sus amigos dan clases de baile los domingos.

Conclusion

We have done so much in four weeks! I'm sure it's been a whirlwind for you. But look at how far you've come. You can now:

- Introduce yourself
- Describe yourself, your friends, and your family
- Talk about your daily life
- Talk about your feelings
- Discuss your hobbies and routines

Not to mention, you have learned the ins and outs of things such as:

- Conjugating regular verbs
- Conjugating irregular verbs
- Telling time
- What it means to speak "formally" or "informally"

With this book, we have aimed to help you move past some of the biggest hurdles students face when learning Spanish – the ever important balance between immersion and practical application.

We know the struggles that are faced on both sides of the classroom. Through incorporating dialogues and detailed, yet easy-to-understand, grammar explanations, we have worked to make the language come alive in a way that helps you, the independent student, learn in both a natural and structured way.

This first book has focused on teaching you things that you will use regularly. Through doing this, you have gained a strong, working foundation of the language.

That doesn't mean you should stop now, though! There's still a lot of Spanish to explore. And we want to be there with you as you continue on your journey.

For starters, you can check out our website at mydailyspanish.com. There, you will find a wealth of resources – everything from grammar explanations to cultural articles, to tips for bringing Spanish into your home and making it even more a part of your everyday life.

Thank you for sticking with us all the way to the end! We hope you got a lot out of this book! We'd love to hear what you think. If you have comments, questions, or suggestions about this book, please let us know by sending us an email at <u>support@ mydailyspanish.com</u>. This will help us to enhance our books and provide you with better learning resources.

Thank you,

My Daily Spanish Team

How to Download the Free Audio Files

The audio files need to be accessed online. No worries though—it's easy!

On your computer, smartphone, iPhone/iPad, or tablet, simply go to this link:

https://mydailyspanish.com/learning-guide-audio

Be careful! If you are going to type the URL on your browser, please make sure to enter it completely and exactly. Otherwise, it will lead you to an incorrect web page.

You should be directed to a web page where you can see the cover of your book.

Below the cover, you will find two "Click here to download the audio" buttons in blue and orange color.

Option 1 (via Google Drive): The blue one will take you to a Google Drive folder. It will allow you to listen to the audio files online or download them from there. Just "Right click" on the track and click "Download." You can also download all the tracks in one click—just look for the "Download all" option.

Option 2 (direct download): The orange button/backup link will allow you to directly download all the files (in .zip format) to your computer.

Note: This is a large file. Do not open it until your browser tells you that it has completed the download successfully (usually a few minutes on a broadband connection, but if your connection is slow it could take longer).

The .zip file will be found in your "Downloads" folder unless you have changed your settings. Extract the .zip file and you will now see all the audio tracks. Save them to your preferred folder or copy them to your other devices. Please play the audio files using a music/Mp3 application.

Did you have any problems downloading the audio? If you did, feel free to send an email to support@mydailyspanish.com. We'll do our best to assist you, but we would greatly appreciate it if you could thoroughly review the instructions first.

Thank you,

My Daily Spanish Team

About My Daily Spanish

MyDailySpanish.com is a website created to help busy learners learn Spanish. It is designed to provide a fun and fresh take on learning Spanish through:

- Helping you create a daily learning habit that you will stick to until you reach fluency, and
- Making learning Spanish as enjoyable as possible for people of all ages.

With the help of awesome content and tried-and-tested language learning methods, My Daily Spanish aims to be the best place on the web to learn Spanish.

The website is continuously updated with free resources and useful materials to help you learn Spanish. This includes grammar and vocabulary lessons plus culture topics to help you thrive in a Spanish-speaking location – perfect not only for those who wish to learn Spanish, but also for travelers planning to visit Spanish-speaking destinations.

For any questions, please email support@mydailyspanish.com.

Thank you,

My Daily Spanish Team

Improve Your Reading and Listening Skills in Spanish

- 11 fun and engaging Spanish stories

- 1,500+ Spanish words and expressions

- Practice your listening and pronunciation skills with the FREE audio — narrated by native Spanish speakers.

LEARN MORE

https://geni.us/spanishbookbeginner